I dedicate this book to my friend and my guide—
Edgar Allan Poe. Thank you for always having faith
in me even when I thought that I lost faith within myself.
But thank you most of all for teaching me that those
who dream by day are cognizant of many things
that escape those who dream only at night.

D1563989

Photo By E.C. Campbell Photography

About the Author

Kristy Robinett (Livonia, MI) is a psychic medium and author who began seeing spirits at the age of three. When she was eight, her deceased grandfather helped her escape from a would-be kidnapper, and it was then that she realized the other side wasn't so far away. As an adult, she is often asked by the local police to examine cold cases. She gained a reputation for being extremely accurate at psychical profiling. She then began working with US law enforcement agencies, attorneys, and private investigators on missing persons, arson, and cold cases. Her psychic detective work was recognized in a new series on the ID Network, *Restless Souls*.

Robinett teaches psychic development and paranormal investigating at local colleges, lectures across the country, and is a regular media commentator. She is the author of *Messenger Between Worlds, Higher Intuitions Oracle, Ghosts of Southeast Michigan,* and *Michigan's Haunted Legends and Lore.* Visit her online at KristyRobinett.com, facebook .com/kristyrobinett, or on Twitter @kristyrobinett.

Kristy Robinett

_____

forevermore

_____

GUIDED IN SPIRIT BY
EDGAR ALLAN POE

Llewellyn Publications
Woodbury, Minnesota

FIRST EDITION
First Printing, 2014

Book design by Bob Gaul
Cover design by Kevin R. Brown
Cover illustration by John Kicksee/The July Group
Cover images: iStockphoto.com/3018275/©dem10
            iStockphoto.com/1977601/©dem10
Editing by Stephanie Finne

Llewellyn Publications is a registered trademark of Llewellyn Worldwide Ltd.

Library of Congress Cataloging-in-Publication Data
Robinett, Kristy.
  Forevermore: guided in spirit by Edgar Allan Poe/Kristy Robinett.
     pages cm
  Includes bibliographical references.
  ISBN 978-0-7387-4067-6
1. Guides (Spiritualism) 2. Poe, Edgar Allan, 1809–1849 (Spirit) 3. Robinett, Kristy—Psychology. I. Title.
  BF1311.P64R63 2014
  133.9'1—dc23
                    2014007948

Llewellyn Publications
A Division of Llewellyn Worldwide Ltd.
2143 Wooddale Drive
Woodbury, MN 55125-2989
www.llewellyn.com

Printed in the United States of America

Contents

Acknowledgments

I admit that I did a lot of soul-searching before I wrote this book. "What will people think?" I asked myself over and over, questioning if this was perhaps career suicide. After all, I think of myself as being abnormally normal in the psychic and mediumship world, and yet here I was writing about having a famous spirit guide. Would I be prepared for the judgment and teasing? I wasn't sure, but what I did know was that the book had to be written and shared. And that couldn't have happened without the help of many people. Thank you...

Thank you to Amy Glaser. I'm grateful that when I queried on the story she didn't think that I was completely insane and continued to support me by wearing an Edgar Allan Poe T-shirt to the vision meeting. She never once blew me off when I anxiously and frequently inquired about this or that. I am very grateful that she believed in me.

Thank you to Ed Day for being a fabulous editor and for going to bat for me at the vision meeting.

To the many radio stations who have loved and promoted me, especially Blaine Fowler and Allyson Martinek of 96.3 WDVD, Detroit, Michigan; Jack and Ron of 98.9 Kiss FM, Oklahoma City, Oklahoma; and Shawn Wild and Kat du Bois originally of Panama City, Florida.

Thank you to Gayle Buchan who has supported and loved me like a best friend and a mother figure. Words cannot describe how much your constant encouragement has helped me find my path.

To Donna Shorkey who came into my life as a client and then as an assistant, but in the end became a best friend. Through her own trials and tragedies, she has always stood by my side without any agenda and always with love and support.

Thank you to Laura Bohlman, Rosalyn Wrobel, Nancie Rowe-Janitz, and Kerry Combs for being wonderful friends and cheerleaders, and to Courtney Sieira for always making my hair look messy fun.

Mary Byberg who met me through a serendipitous encounter and who is the most patient and loving friend and assistant that I could ask for. I am eternally grateful.

Billy Sanders and Michael Griffith of the Reynolds Mansion, who shared their beautiful B & B with Chuck and me and who didn't think I was too nuts when I randomly called them out of the blue. And to Shary Connella for taking awesome photos and helping continue my connection to the mansion.

Thanks to Debi Martone for her help in reading and editing my manuscript before I handed it over to the publisher. I am incredibly grateful for her creativity and her honesty.

Jenni Licata and Jennifer Hupke—my goddesses of the abnormally normal. With your friendship and our blog the Majickal Life (http://themajickallife.blogspot.com/), you've helped me with an outlet that simply helped me embrace the gifts that I always knew I had but never had the support to share. It has taken me a long time to confess who I truly am, what I truly am, and even then I grow each day within the identity of who I am and who I want to be. The years haven't been without trials and tribulations, but through all of the negative, and with your help, I always saw the rainbow through the rain, and I continue to.

My husband, Chuck Robinett, kids Micaela Even and Connor Even, and stepdaughters Cora Robinett and Molly Robinett. It isn't easy having me as a wife or a mom, but it is rare for any of them to complain even when I say that I think we need to take a trip, or that we need to visit a cemetery down a darkened dirt road. They've blindly and with endless trust came along with me on my journey, and I love each one of them so much.

To my clients, my friends, readers, listeners, and fans who have stood by my side through life's crazy ride. Without you and all your love and support, this book would not have been written.

To all the law enforcement agencies that I've worked with and who've tirelessly poured over cases. And to all of the families of the missing and murdered. There will forever be a place in my heart for and with you.

To my mom, Sally Schiller, on the other side who shared her love of reading and literature with me, and to my dad, Ronald Schiller, who I share a birthday with, along with his stubbornness and perseverance.

Introduction

One of my first memories, at the age of two, is of my own spirit guides. My parents and siblings referred to them as my imaginary friends, but to me they were real and still are. They have names and physical features, they're not transparent like what is shown in movies. I could—and still can—see them, feel them, and hear them. I believe that everybody can connect with their guides, they just need to understand how.

My first guide announced himself as Alto, a Native American Indian with tanned skin and long, shiny, raven-black hair. Although most of the time he displays a serious look on his face, his gentle brown eyes show his softer side. Dressed in tanned hide pants and a colorful jacket, he wears many necklaces, bracelets, and even earrings. There are no tattoos or paintings on his skin, and no headdress. My main protector and spirit guard and guide, he helps inspire and encourage me through every challenge life throws my way.

I cannot count how many times I have apologized to him for being frustrating and hardheaded.

My second guide, an Irish beauty named Tallie, has shoulder-length, red, curly hair. Her blue-green eyes sparkle like calming water. Tallie has a peaceful demeanor and a sophisticated sense of humor. Her love of literature, music, and nature help to ground me and steer me to beautiful things. She has also been the one who helped with love and lost love.

And then when I was thirteen years old, another guide presented himself to me. His name is Edgar Allan Poe.

Everybody has a spirit guide (or guides), whether known or wanted, assigned to us before we are even born. Guides are people who have once lived on the earthly plane, experienced love, heartache, and all emotions life has to offer. They are responsible for guiding us through our life and leading us on the best path with the least amount of karma.

Chosen through vibration or through our own higher selves, a guide would be someone who, if alive in this earthly plane, you would get along with famously. They aren't necessarily famous (but they could be). If you have ever gone into a grocery store and a complete stranger comes up and talks to you, and during those brief moments you have a connection—that is vibrational alignment. The same goes for those you meet and your first and final impression is that you just don't like them. Your guide is vibrationally aligned to you.

Some guides are with you throughout your lifetime, and some are transitional guides who show up to assist you in specific areas of your life for a specific reason. If you are going through medical issues, you may have a guide who had been a nurse or a doctor in their earthly life, or had gone through the same medical issue. If you are going through love issues, a guide may join your team who had a long and successful marriage, or maybe was a marriage counselor. There is always a logical reason behind each spirit guide. Guides guide with what they learned on the earthly plane. When we cross over, we choose our job. So if you thought you'd be floating around in the clouds playing the cello or harp, you are sadly mistaken. Well, unless you are a musician now and will be assisting a fellow musician as a guide. So there is an even greater incentive to learn and grow now as it follows you even into death.

What I didn't know at the age of thirteen was the impact that Edgar Allan Poe would have on my life and continues to have. It had nothing to do with his writings or pressure to channel him and write, although it certainly hasn't hurt. In his life, Poe stood for justice and yet received anything but. So in this lifetime, through me, we uncover truths of the past, what some may call macabre—murder, suicide, perceived accidents—that have found their way into this lifetime. I have always been a reluctant psychic and medium, but Poe has been an encouraging and insightful guide, especially with missing persons cases. His insight has been integral in assisting me with trusting my own gut instincts along with channeling his confidence.

As much as he would love to say that we solve them, I give full credit to law enforcement. However, it doesn't take away from the fact that this insightful guide and sleuth, a man often called a lunatic, is far from mad. With his assistance, we peer into the darkness to shine a light on the wrongs that have found their way into this lifetime.

Edgar Allan Poe walked me through his life, which intersected with my own past life—a life that I knew was there, but didn't know to what extent. It is said that we repeat lives if we haven't fulfilled something from the past. Poe helped me not only discover what I missed in a long-ago time by taking me on his own journey of life and death, but he helped me put my soul pieces back together in order to help others with their own life-and-death mystery.

Poe experienced much turmoil in his life and went on to die misunderstood. His bitterness shines through the cracks of the leather-bound poems and literature. But as we are all given the chance to perceive our life in-depth from the other side, we learn and we grow, if we choose to. We can then go on to help others who are going through similar experiences. Edgar Allan Poe (and other divinity) decided to use me as a vessel not just to share his experiences, but to experience them with him so that I may share with you as I was guided in spirit by Edgar Allan Poe.

chapter one

– October 1984 –

"No!" he screamed at me, flailing his arms in my face. "No, that will not do."

"Seriously?" I rolled my eyes and began to raise my voice, but instead I muttered under my breath. As if I didn't have enough problems with the living, the dead were also critiquing me. "What were you assigned to me for again, Edgar? Umm, Mr. Poe?" I stammered. Honestly, what do you call the ghost of one of the best gothic horror authors? And how could I yell at a historical figure who was trying to help me? But then again, this man was known for being unstable, and I was starting to feel as if he was making me a bit nuts.

My English assignment was due in the morning, I was tired and crabby, and I just so happened to have the spirit of a famous author haunting me. Well, not necessarily haunting—he was supposed to be guiding me—

but I felt more like I was in a really bad *Candid Camera* episode. Or maybe *America's Funniest Home Videos*. Whatever was happening couldn't be real. It couldn't be true. But it was.

"*Edgar* will do just fine," Poe muttered, plopping on my pink plaid comforter and staring at my lavender colored walls, obviously as unhappy with the assignment as I was.

Instead of feeling as if he was helping me in any way, shape, or form, I wondered how I was karmically chosen, or doomed, to babysit a madman.

"I am to assist you with your writing, amongst other things, but I'm not so sure even the genius that I am will be able to help."

"So you're saying I'm a lost cause?" I felt crushed and the tone of my voice reflected it.

The spirit slowly sat up on my twin-size bed and gave me a hard look, one eyebrow raised, as if my question jarred a memory. My gray tabby, Silver, jumped up on the bed next to Poe, and he mindlessly began to pet him, still lost in thought.

"Why you?" I lashed out. "Honestly, I think I need Einstein. I'm almost failing math and yet I'm getting As in English. Is it possible to do a trade like they do in sports?"

Frustrated and emotionally depleted, I slammed my pencil down on my Trapper Keeper, pushed my chair away from my whitewashed desk, and rushed to the bathroom where I began to cry.

"If it makes you feel any better, I was expelled from the University because of my failure to do math. That and my father stopped paying my tuition and I became a pauper."

"No, no, that doesn't make me feel better," I moaned, sniffling. *Nobody will believe this. I will for sure get thrown into a psychiatric ward,* I thought.

"Kristy!" I heard my mom calling from the bottom of the stairwell. "Kristy, are you okay?"

I quickly blew my nose and cleared my throat before opening the bathroom door. "Yeah, Mom, just frustrated with homework," I replied, trying to sound normal.

My mom had lost her eyesight the year before, when I was about twelve years old. Although she couldn't see more than dark shadows, her other senses, including her psychic sense, were quite keen. A slight lift in my voice would set them off that I was crying, and I didn't want to deal with explaining anything to her. She had her own issues, most of them mourning her mom, dad, and brothers who had all passed away within several years of one another, leaving her feeling orphaned. Then her various ailments ultimately led her sight to fade completely away. I couldn't blame her, really. I tried to stay out of her hair as best as I could, even being a hormonal, thirteen-year-old Scorpio with a short temper, especially when it came to critical spirits.

"Okay," she replied, hesitantly.

I could hear her taking a puff of her cigarette, something that frightened me to no end. Without her sight, she was known to light the wrong end of the cigarette, let the ashes grow too long where they would fall on the floor, or just set down the cigarette in odd places and forget about it. I was sure that one day the house would just burst into flames, and it scared me.

"Dinner will be ready in about a half an hour."

Cube steak again more than likely. I sighed. "I'll be down in a few minutes."

I felt trapped. If I went into my bedroom I had to deal with an erratic and ornery spirit. Or I could go downstairs and deal with constant questions about my truly humdrum life, albeit minus specters, from my mom who was just bored and looking for some excitement, even if it came from me.

I screamed in frustration and slammed my fists on the canary yellow sink, which hurt. I cried, but this time the tears were because I bruised my hands on the porcelain. Maybe, just maybe, I could break my hand, or maybe just a finger, and not be able to write at all. That would solve the Poe problem. I wouldn't be able to write and therefore he would have to go haunt someone else. I laughed at the crazy thought and instead took a washcloth off the mirrored shelf, wet it with warm water, and washed my tear-streaked face. Taking a deep breath, I walked out of the bathroom and down the steps to dinner. Poe would just have to wait.

Dinner was the same routine—Dad sat in his chair, television blasting, eating, while Mom and I sat at the dining room table and complained about Dad sitting in his chair, eating, with the television blasting. If ever there was a loop in time, I felt as if I were caught in it.

An hour or so later, I quietly walked back into my room and looked around to see if there might be a spirit or two hanging around. But to my delight, it looked to be in the clear.

I plopped on my bed and stared at the white ceiling. The difficulty of being a teenager, and then being a teenager who could see into the afterlife, was something of a curse most of the time.

I was only three years old when a family member on the other side came through with a prediction of death, a prediction that would come true. Apparently a door was left open afterward, because soon after I became inundated with what my family called imaginary friends, yet not all of them were friendly. No, I wasn't just talking about the spirit of the famous horror writer; it was even more dark and dreary than that, and something Edgar Allan Poe would write about, if alive.

I was actually petrified of my room and my house. It was as if a dark shadow loomed about and as soon as I walked through the door I felt as if I was being pulled into an abyss of negativity. Everybody felt it when they entered, even though the home looked like a typical house from the outside. And even though I begged my parents to move, my dad was bound and determined that he wouldn't be driven out of his house by what he thought was pure paranoia. My room wasn't any haven either. Instead, it felt like a breeding ground for ghosts, where there was a constant elevator from the other side—and that side wasn't necessarily a pleasant place.

I heard a knock on the front door and then heard someone climbing the thirteen steps to the second floor.

"Boo!" my best friend Deanna said as she came in.

"Funny."

Even though Deanna was my best friend for many years and had heard of each and every crush, had commiserated with me through every fight that I had with my mom, and had even vacationed with me, she didn't know the full extent of my psychic abilities. If she did, she would have probably thought her entrance was even funnier than it was.

"What ya working on?" She peeked over at my homework.

"English. It's a poetry assignment and I'm supposed to profess my undying love in it." I pretended to gag. "I have never really been in love, so how realistic can this get?"

"Easy peasy," Deanna laughed and pointed at one of the many posters that graced my walls. "Pretend it's for Jon over there."

Poe stood leaning against my very loud flowered wall-papered metal closet looking skeptically at my best friend. "With me, poetry has not been a purpose, but a passion," I heard him say telepathically.

I thought for a second. "Not a bad idea," I said, looking at Bon Jovi's picture with his long, frizzy, blond-highlighted hair blowing in the wind. "Okay, I'm feeling like I have a muse, Dee. Thanks! I'll give you a call later."

"Glad I could help!" Deanna smiled, lightly brushed her shoulder as if to congratulate herself, and bounced down the steps. "Bye, Mr. and Mrs. Schiller. See you tomorrow."

I heard the door close, grabbed my pencil that had a dancing Snoopy on it, and began to feel the inspiration of love pour out on the notepaper. Poe stood silently in the corner of my room, his left brow furled and exasperated. We obviously had a lot to learn from one another.

Within the matter of an hour, my assignment was complete and I felt proud and content. Poe looked over my shoulder at the final piece and just muttered, "Indescribable," which I took as acceptance.

Love Scattered

Scattered on the ground your love is lost there.
I walk picking them up, but the winds do blow.
My hands are emptied feeling alone and bare.
In a dark garden, the sun shines without care.
Lost on a sorrowful road near a meadow.

Scattered on the ground your love is lost there.
Among the green leaves and flowers so faire,
A gloomy garden blooms in bright yellow.
My hands are emptied feeling alone and bare.
Without notice the weather turns dark around the lair.
The winds turn violent and bough the willow.

Scattered on the ground your love is lost there.
Afraid and lonely, the road leads to nowhere.
The lightning and thunder set the sky aglow.

My hands are emptied feeling alone and bare,
unknown to what will happen after this affair.

Looking down the new road shines a rainbow.
Scattered on the ground your love is lost there.
My hands are emptied feeling alone and bare.

"Love lost," he said in more of a statement than a question. "You know, Kristy, you remind me of someone from my past…" He bit his lip and closed his eyes, as if replaying scenes from a faraway time.

Grabbing some pink nail polish from my desk drawer, I began to give myself a manicure. "Who would that be?"

"Her name was Sara," Poe began, but before he could go any further, I gasped and spilled my nail polish on my desk. As I ran to get some towels from the bathroom, I wondered if his assignment to me might actually have a method to the madness, or maybe just more madness to the madness.

I wiped up the nail polish and cussed under my breath at the smear on my thumbnail, frustrated that I would have to begin all over again.

"Edgar, did you say Sara? Did you know that I always, from the very beginning of time, believed my name to be Sara and not Kristy?"

Poe only nodded.

Since I was two years old, I would tell my family over and over again that my name wasn't Kristy but Sara. They never understood, nor did I, but I knew deep in my soul that the current time and place was not *my* true time and place.

"Am I...her?" My eyes grew wide as I awaited his answer.

Poe let out a thoughtful sigh and shook his head. "I'm not sure. Maybe. Probably not though."

Poe looked as if he was about to add something, but he stopped himself.

"I don't think I believe in reincarnation anyway," I pondered.

"You don't think you believe in reincarnation, Kristy, or were you told that there was no such thing as reincarnation?"

He had a point. I was enrolled in a Lutheran school, and we were taught that ghosts, spirits, psychics, mediums, and reincarnation were of the devil. Well, I didn't think I was of the devil, although my parents might have disagreed every so often. So why would reincarnation be any different?

I had a lot to think about and to research.

Two days later, before classes started, I went to the school library. My English teacher, Mrs. Bird, was sitting at the checkout desk grading what looked like our poetry papers.

"Kristy, can I help you?" she asked.

She sounded aggravated, but I had gotten up early for a reason. Normally, I would've just told her never mind but my curiosity was bubbling.

"Yes, Mrs. Bird, are there any books on Edgar Allan Poe here that I can borrow? Not books he wrote, but on his life?"

She gave me a crooked look, got up, walked to the biography section, pulled out two books, and handed them to me.

"I just read your poem, Kristy, and I'm wondering where you got it from."

"I wrote it, Mrs. Bird," I said, confused.

"Hmm, it's good. I thought perhaps you copied it from somewhere."

I was appalled. My cheeks began to turn red in both anger and embarrassment. "No, Mrs. Bird, I wrote it. My mom and dad can attest to that."

"I may have to call them. I will see you in class, Kristy."

She may have to call them? How could she even think that I copied it? I had never gotten in trouble before and I was getting in trouble for doing an assignment?!

Mrs. Bird did in fact call and my mom informed her that I spent several hours writing the poem. Even Deanna told her that I was working on it when she came over, but I don't think she believed Dee, my mom, or me. It was going to be a long year.

After I got home from school and complained to my mom about how unfair I thought I was being treated, I was able to sit down and read more about my mysterious guide, with the hopes of understanding why he was even assigned to me in the first place.

chapter Two

As I read through the books on Edgar Allan Poe that I had checked out of the school's library, I saw several synchronicities between our lives: I was thirteen when Poe was assigned to me (which was the age of Virginia when they married); I also had two siblings; and I loved to write, especially poetry. No, it wasn't enough to connect all the dots, but it made Poe mortal.

I sunk my teeth into the sordid stories of his love life. I realized that even though he came across as cynical and sassy and, to some, dark and macabre, he wore his heart on his sleeve and had been put through the ringer with so much love lost.

Edgar Allan Poe was born on January 19, 1809, to traveling actors in Boston. He was the second of three children and was only two years old when his biological parents passed away. He was taken in by the wealthy tobacco merchant John Allan and his wife Frances Valentine

Allan in Richmond, Virginia. Poe's older brother and younger sister went to live with other families.

Mr. Allan had high hopes that Poe would follow in his footsteps as a tobacco businessman. But Poe had an early love of poetry and writing and by the age of thirteen had enough works of poetry to publish a book, but his headmaster advised Mr. Allan against doing it.

In 1826, Poe attended the University of Virginia, where he was an excellent student. But Poe's heart never sang when it came to school; instead he loved creative writing. Because his foster father was so disappointed in his life choice of the arts, he stopped paying for his schooling and left Poe with a considerable amount of debt. Desperate, Poe turned to gambling in order to pay off his bills. Obviously a bad gambler, by the end of his first term, Poe was so poor that he had to burn his furniture in order to keep warm. He became bitter and angry at Allan for not providing enough money.

Before attending the University of Virginia, Poe had fallen in love with and proposed to Elmira Royster. However, upon his return to Richmond for a visit, he discovered that Elmira was engaged to another. Betrayed by the woman he loved and unable to take the constant fighting between him and his father, he set out to accomplish what he wanted to do most—write and publish a book and join the military. He did just that.

On May 26, 1827, Poe enlisted in the US army as a private using a false name and age—Edgar A. Perry, twenty-two years old—even though he was only eighteen.

Poe's regiment was sent to Charleston, South Carolina, and he was promoted to artificer, with a raise that doubled his monthly salary. But as history would once again repeat, Poe grew bored after attaining the rank of sergeant-major for artillery (the highest rank a noncommissioned officer can achieve). He came clean to his commanding lieutenant, confessing his true identity and age and asking to be discharged three years early. His lieutenant told him the only way he would allow an early release was if Poe reconciled with his father, John Allan, and wrote a letter of apology.

Poe wrote to Allan, but it was several months before his father responded. He wrote to tell Poe that the only mother he had ever known, Frances Allan, was dying of tuberculosis and wanted to see him before she died. By the time Poe got home, Frances had died and had been buried. Through grief, Poe and Allan briefly reconciled. Allan even helped Poe gain an appointment to the US Military Academy at West Point.

Before going to West Point, Poe published another volume of poetry and was basking in his accomplishment when he heard that his father remarried without even telling him. He took out a pen and paper and poured his heart out to Allan, detailing all that he felt Allan did wrong. Allan obviously didn't take it well and burned all bridges, including having Poe thrown out of West Point. Poe returned to Baltimore, broke and lonely. This time Poe's aunt Maria Clemm welcomed him into her home, and she became like a mother to him.

While Poe was in Baltimore, Allan died and left Poe out of his will. Instead, Allan provided for an illegitimate child he had never seen.

Poe continued to write, entering writing contests and applying for newspaper positions. Although he was living in poverty, he was persistent and finally found himself in an editorial position at the *Southern Literary Messenger* in Richmond, Virginia. It was at that magazine that he found his love as a magazine writer. He worked hard to make it one of the most popular magazines in the south. With sensational stories and scathing book reviews, he earned a reputation as a son of a gun and began to collect many enemies within his field. He didn't much care, though, and finally felt in charge of his life for once.

At the age of twenty-seven, he moved Maria and Virginia Clemm to Richmond and married Virginia, who was just thirteen. Poe finally had the carefree and loving life that he so wanted. Even though he still wasn't earning sufficient money, during the day he wrote and at night he doted on a woman whom he loved. He was surrounded by a family he longed for and his evenings were filled with piano playing and singing.

Poe's life seemed to be settled, but once again he grew to be unsatisfied. Due to low pay and lack of editorial control, Poe left his job and moved to New York City in the wake of the financial crisis known as the Panic of 1837. Poe struggled to find magazine work and instead spent time writing novels, which weren't being sold. In 1838, after only a year in New York, Poe moved to Philadelphia and wrote for a number of different magazines, where he finally began to receive the accolades and the fame that he strived for. But that didn't come without a high price, both in a monetary sense and ego. Poe was beginning to accumulate many enemies along his course to stardom. He didn't much care about that. Instead, the deep poverty was affecting his male ego. His soul only found solace at home with his wife and mother-in-law, until tragedy struck again.

In 1841, his wife, Virginia, contracted tuberculosis, the disease that had already claimed Poe's mother, brother, and his foster mother. Poe became even more determined to be successful, and he moved back to New York in 1844. It was there that he wrote a story on a balloon trip around the world. It became a huge sensation and set everyone abuzz until Poe confessed it was all just a hoax. No matter, the sham helped to make Poe a household name until he released the poem, "The Raven" in January 1845, which made him famous. He held lectures and began to receive the pay that he thought he deserved. However, Poe's notoriety was short-lived. A year later, with a failed magazine venture, rumors of an extramarital affair, and deteriorating health of his wife, Poe left New York. He took refuge in a small country cottage, where Virginia passed away in 1847.

Everyone assumed Poe would drink himself to death. He surprised even his critics when he began traveling from one city to the next, giving lectures and petitioning investors for his newest magazine idea.

While on a lecture tour in Massachusetts, Poe met and befriended Nancy Richmond. He was taken with her poetry, but since she was married, he moved on to poetess Sarah Helen Whitman, who lived in Providence.

Whitman and Poe first met in July 1845 at a lecture. Whitman was attracted to Poe and admired him, so she asked to be introduced. Poe declined. As he left the lecture, Poe saw Whitman standing in her rose garden. In 1848, a friend of Whitman's asked her to write a poem for a Valentine's Day party. Whitman wrote the poem titled, "To Edgar Allan Poe." Poe heard about it, and, being quite full of himself, the two began a relationship through notes and poems. Three months into the courtship, Poe wrote Whitman the poem "To Helen," referencing the moment when he first saw her in the rose garden. From then on he referred to her as Sarah Helen after the poem he so lovingly wrote for her.

In December 1848, Poe proposed marriage and Whitman agreed with one stipulation—that he remain sober. Poe agreed and they set the wedding date for just a few weeks later. But Poe broke his promise only a few days after making it by hitting the bottle. Whitman's mother also found out that Poe was still pursuing Nancy Richmond and childhood sweetheart Elmira Royster Shelton. The wedding was called off, apparently just the day beforehand, when he went on yet another drunken rampage. Many believe that he had cold feet and had done it purposefully.

Soon after, Poe was reunited with his first fiancée Elmira Royster Shelton in Richmond, who was now widowed, and he began to court her. He believed himself engaged when he left for Philadelphia to help edit a poem for a colleague. Along the way, he stopped in Baltimore.

On October 3, 1849, Joseph W. Walker found Poe wandering the streets of Baltimore in clothes that weren't his own and sent a note to Dr. J. E. Snodgrass stating that he found Edgar Allan Poe at Ryan's 4th Ward Polls in distress and needing immediate assistance.

Baltimore City, Oct. 3, 1849

Dear Sir,

There is a gentleman, rather the worse for wear, at Ryan's 4th ward polls, who goes under the cognomen of Edgar A. Poe, and who appears in great distress, & he says he is acquainted with you, he is in need of immediate assistance.

Yours, in haste,
JOS. W. WALKER

To Dr. J. E. Snodgrass.

Ryan's 4th Ward Polls was a tavern where elections were often held. Instead of a sticker or a pin denoting that you voted, as we have today, you received a drink. Dr. Snodgrass and Poe's uncle, Henry Herring, arrived at the tavern and agreed that Poe should be sent to Washington College Hospital. They believed that Poe was in a drunken stupor and would just sleep it off, not even bothering to alert his new fiancée or mother-in-law. After several days of slipping in and out of consciousness, when they asked Poe what happened, he whispered the name "Reynolds." On October 7, 1849, depending on which account one accepts, Poe died at about 3:00 a.m. or 5:00 a.m. at the age of forty. His last words were "Lord, help my poor soul." His cause of death was ascribed to "congestion of the brain," however no autopsy was performed. Edgar Allan Poe was buried in Baltimore two days later.

To this day, the exact cause of Poe's death remains a mystery.

At least that was what the books all say. There are over twenty theories on how Edgar Allan Poe died, including rabies, diabetes, epilepsy, carbon monoxide poisoning, alcohol, and everything in between.

———

"Want to know the truth?" Poe grinned and fixed the collar on his coat.

"No, that's okay," I nonchalantly answered, putting the books in my denim school bag.

He drew closer. "What do you mean with 'that's okay'? I always liked a good whodunit, and my death," Poe puffed his chest out, "is one of the best, I might add."

"So you tell me how you died, Edgar, and who am I going to tell? Better yet, who is going to believe me?"

I really was quite curious as to the whole story, the true story, but I wasn't so sure he would offer me the truth. He was a writer, a poet, a tale teller, and I wasn't confident that he wouldn't elaborate. And, as I had asked him, so I become privy to history-changing information and what was I to do with it exactly?

"One day I will tell you, Kristy. No, I will show you. There is a reason that I am your guide." Edgar pondered for a moment. "Oh, I do love abstruseness, but only when I write it!"

"I didn't get a position on the paper," I confessed, changing the subject.

"What do you mean you weren't given a position?"

"She just doesn't like me, Edgar."

It was my sophomore year of high school and I had decided that I wanted to be part of the school newspaper. But the teacher wasn't allowing that to happen. It was the very same teacher who called my parents the previous year on the poem she was so sure I copied from somewhere.

"She gave me absolutely no criticism, just said that I wasn't a good fit. This is the same lady who gave me a D in typing because my typewriter stopped working and I couldn't make it up after class. And this from the same lady who wouldn't even give me a stagehand position in the play. She just doesn't like me," I said, feeling rejected.

"Humph, well, I know all about that, my dear. Critics. There are many, and you have to be prepared for a life of constant judgment."

Constant? I silently groaned. I wanted to be loved, not hated. Judgment is rarely fun, and I didn't have thick skin.

"She even thinks that I plagiarized my last poem." I sniffed back tears.

Poe's face turned dark and he thrust his hands in his pockets. "I do hate those who plagiarize. I used to call them out in my reviews. Oh, and Kristy, there were many, don't let the history books tell you differently! But you, my dear, you I saw staring at that odd-looking man." Poe pointed to my poster of Jon Bon Jovi that was taped right next to my poster of RATT. "And, well, you didn't plagiarize."

"So what do I do now, Edgar?"

"Not what I did. The reverse, actually." He sat down on my bed, looking pensive.

"I'm thinking that my mom and dad would kill me if I started drinking or taking opium. And actually, how did you write such fine literature when you were always lushing it up?"

Poe looked up at me and shook his head. Sadness seemed to vibrate within his energy.

"I didn't drink that much," Poe said as I snickered back at him. "Honest."

"Still in denial, or ...?"

"I drank. There is no denying that, but I had a very low tolerance of alcohol, so only one drink would have me intoxicated. My stepfather, or father as I was to call him, beat me. He beat me incessantly. The wounds were mostly on my back, but there were frequent times that I was hit in the head. Whether it was the beatings or the emotional abuse, I don't know, but I remember these horrible head-aches. I suppose they now call them migraines. When I entered my teenage years, I would do anything to make them go away, and most of the time that was with alcohol. So between the hurt head and the liquor, I suppose I did look like a raging alcoholic."

I had a pretty keen intuitiveness for liars, and I could tell that he was being truthful.

"And opium?"

Poe shook his head, "I was offered opium for my head-aches, and I took it once and only once. I was not an addict like many wanted to—and maybe still do—believe. I have absolutely no pleasure in the stimulants in which I some-times so madly indulge. It has not been in the pursuit of pleasure that I have periled life and reputation and reason. It has been the desperate attempt to escape from torturing memories, from a sense of insupportable loneliness, and a dread of some strange impending doom."

"You never sought any further medical assistance?"

"I didn't trust people in general, and never doctors. They never healed anyone I loved, so what good were they? And if they were to see my old wounds, rumors would start. It was easier to run away and drink."

"I'm sorry, Edgar."

He just shrugged. "I was never really insane except upon occasions when my heart was touched."

I was born cursed, or gifted, however you wanted to define it, with the ability to see ghosts and spirits. It became apparent at the age of three when my so-called imaginary friends didn't go away and had detailed information that they had me share with my parents, which could be validated. When my great-grandmother in spirit came through to tell me that her daughter, my grandma, was going to die, and then six months later she did, my mom didn't take the imaginary friends as lightly as she and the rest of my family had before. It wasn't all fun and cute after I predicted death.

I was raised from birth by a father who started his day with his weathered, leather-bound Bible in his lap while sipping his morning coffee and who said a prayer before each meal. After my prediction at the age of four, my parents enrolled me at the local Lutheran school. I was now taught in school and at home that anything to do with spirits, ghosts, and even reading horoscopes were huge no-nos. So how ironic was it that I was placed in a household of paranormal nonbelievers and naysayers being able to see, hear, feel, and know that which was unexplained? Not only was I able to build a relationship with my spirit guides, but I lived between the thin line of two worlds. And so did my house.

The Victorian house in Detroit, Michigan, was what was called home, yet felt anything but homey. The house had a haunted history, with frequent unexplained occurrences: shadows that lurked, voices that could be heard through the radio and television despite them being shut off, phone calls in the middle of the night with heavy breathing, temperature changes, and a feeling of being watched.

My bedroom seemed to be one of the hot spots for the most paranormal activity. I hated my bedroom, most of the time sleeping on the living room couch, but spending my afternoons in my room doing homework and watching television. Even in the daylight you could feel a darkness that loomed over the house.

I never knew why the house was so paranormally active. With my mom so afraid of anything ghostly and my dad such a skeptic, I didn't know what was true or not. I heard whispers that my siblings once played with an Ouija Board in the home. During their attempted contact, the planchette flew across the room, which frightened them. My mom made them put the board in the garbage, only for it to show back up in the room later that night. Another rumor was that a man was killed in the basement because of a bitter argument from a love triangle. No matter how it happened, or why it happened, the house had an evil energy that was disruptive. It was as if a black cloud hovered over the house and the sun shined around it and nothing ever moved that black cloud away, it just got darker and darker day by day, year by year.

Other than Poe, I had several other guides who had been assisting me since birth, including a Native American named Alto and a pretty Irish lady named Tallie. But like most everything else in life, we all have free will and free choice, which means that I didn't have to listen or take their advice. What a frustrating job for them. I always wished that they could assist with the paranormal activity and thought perhaps Poe, due to his haunting works, was assigned to me because of my magnetism *from* the supernatural, and ultimately *to* the supernatural.

"Edgar, do you see the ghosts that haunt me—that haunt this house?" I inquired, licking my grape lip-glossed lips.

"Whether it is a house, or a soul, we forever remain haunted," he replied ominously and disappeared.

Poe was different from my other guides. My other guides rarely communicated with me unless I inquired upon something or needed help. Poe, apparently, was still coloring outside the lines of the norm, bucking the system even when it came to the other side. I didn't feel as if he was necessarily guiding me, but almost felt as if I was guiding him, which made me wonder if he was truly a guide or more of a ghost.

Ghosts are different than spirits, a misconception rarely taught. We all have souls and spirits, so we have a choice when we die to cross over or to continue to visit our loved ones. Once we cross, we become a spirit. But there are a few who are afraid of judgment once they cross, they don't want to leave their family, or possibly they just miss the boat, err, I mean light, and they then become a ghost.

Maybe Poe was right. Maybe it wasn't the house that was haunted, but my soul, and maybe it had something to do with a past life, or lives. In school we had just begun studying Buddhism (yes, even in Lutheran schools we studied other religions), karma, and past lives. Maybe that was why he came through right then. Maybe I had a karmic lesson to learn. Or maybe he still did.

Eh, it was too deep for a thirteen-year-old. I just wanted to crush on boys, read romance novels, and go bowling. Instead, I was pouring over biographies of a dead poet and pondering life's mysteries when I hadn't even had many years of which to ponder.

At least in this lifetime.

I knew from an early age that I didn't quite fit in. My brother always told me that I was dropped off by an alien spaceship, and I don't think he was too off the mark. I didn't look like anyone in my family, I saw spirits from the early age of three, and I wasn't a typical kid. I lived in the city but ached to be in the country. I dreamed of old farmhouses with big, wraparound porches, a barn overflowing with kittens, and a Dutch oven filled with cut up, homegrown vegetables cooking over a fireplace. Instead of Barbie, I would rather play with rag dolls, Holly Hobbie being my favorite. My mom would laugh and ask if I was watching too much *Little House on the Prairie*, but I rarely watched television and would rather read, except for one of my favorite shows—*Dark Shadows*, a gothic soap opera that followed strange happenings to the Collins family from Maine. The show featured vampires, witches, werewolves, and other supernatural creatures, and also had dream sequences that went back in time to the 1800s, alluding to past lives.

It was right up my alley. And probably Poe's, too.

chapter three

Soon after Poe came on the scene as my guide, my life became busy, so busy that my guides became like lost stuffed animals pushed into a toy chest. Between schoolwork, dance classes, sports practices, friends, an ailing mom, and my great need to be out of my haunted house as much as possible, along with trying like mad to be seen as normal, I shunned and attempted to ignore most anything paranormal or metaphysical. Until I had kids myself. Then it was as if the toy chest, or Pandora's Box, was once again opened.

Poe didn't abandon me—I abandoned him, along with the remainder of my spirit guide gang. But it was Poe who I would often find sitting with my mom as she cried and worried. Sometimes I would see him holding her hand, as if trying to console her sadness and gloom. Both my mom and Poe (in life) had lost their parents and siblings, and both of them would surround themselves with the depression that they couldn't see the rainbows through the fog. I

31

couldn't tell if Poe's sympathy helped my mom, but I never believed that it hurt. I saw a similarity between Poe and my mom and wondered why he wasn't guiding her. They both loved family, they both worried about money excessively, and they both loved music. In fact, Poe would often tell me that I needed to play the piano.

"Oh, Kristy, look at your lovely fingers. Those are piano-playing fingers, there."

When I inquired to my mom about taking piano lessons, she would make excuses about how the house was too small for a piano and she didn't have the money for the instrument or the lessons. Ironically, right after my piano suggestion my dad bought me a drum set and took me for lessons.

At twenty-one years of age, I married my high school sweetheart, who disbelieved in the very person that I was. So I tried with all my might to keep the lid tightly closed and padlocked on the gift that I had. I silenced any mention of spirit guides. That was until I was pregnant and had a two-year-old daughter of my own. Then it became harder and harder to ignore and hide.

"Mommy, remember when we died?" my two-year-old daughter, Micaela, asked me nonchalantly as we both sat down on the carpet, playing a memory game.

Everybody thinks that their child is a genius, but Micaela was so far ahead of everyone in her age bracket that it was scary. She learned how to crawl out of her crib when she was just over six months old, began walking when she was nine months old, and was talking in sentences before she should have—her first word *money,* the second *daddy.* The pediatrician, an elderly man with years of experience, would laugh and shake his head, saying that in all his years he had never seen anything like it and wished us luck with a loving pat to our backs.

My eyes slightly squinted at her as I attempted to answer the question. "Micaela, mommy is right here. I'm not dead. Do you even know what *dead* is?"

Micaela flipped over two matching cards and looked up at me with her big, blue eyes. "Dead means that you leave your family and spend time with Jesus, Mommy."

"But I'm right here, honey. And Jesus, well, he is in our hearts, but I am spending time with you right here, right now."

She shook her head, beginning to get agitated. "Mommy, you died in the fire and daddy saved me and my brother." She pointed to my three-month-old pregnant stomach. "I was burned, though," she said, lifting her long, blond ponytail and turning around to show me her birthmark.

Micaela was born with a strawberry patch right by her hairline in the back of her head. "Mic, that is your angel kiss, not a burn."

Micaela giggled, "Angels don't kiss, Mommy!"

We didn't know the sex of the baby, but I had a strong feeling it was a boy. What got me was that as a child I had a fear of fire. I would scream if we went to a restaurant that had candles, and I couldn't leave a room that had a fireplace going, afraid that an ember might jump and start a house fire.

"Where did this happen? Where did Mommy die, Micaela."

"Japan."

It was almost as if the memory acted as a release for her because she grabbed her baby blanket, crawled up on the couch, and fell asleep—something very unlike my daughter.

When her dad got home, I asked what shows he was watching with her, trying to convince myself that she subconsciously saw something that made her weave a story like that.

"Uh, *Barney* and *Blue's Clues*," he responded, puzzled.

Not quite certain how to approach the subject of her conversation, I just dove right in. His response was exactly as I thought it would be—one of disbelief and amusement, most of which was aimed at me for processing it as something possible.

"Yeah, I thought it was odd, too," I said, leaving it at that until a month later. When I found out that I was having a baby boy, I briefly revisited the conversation.

"Don't you think that it is odd that Micaela knew I was having a baby boy?" I asked my husband over lunch.

"She had a fifty-fifty chance, Kristy," he responded skeptically.

It wasn't just her past life memory or the prediction of a baby boy, but just as I had so-called imaginary friends that drove my parents nuts, so did Micaela. But being that I was a medium, I could see them. When kids babble on and on and point, most parents laugh and think it's cute, or wonder if their child might be talking to angels. Well, I could actually *see* who she was talking to.

My own childhood experiences with spirit activity and guides began to flood back as the toy chest that I thought I had locked was pried open. But this time it was not for me, it was for Micaela. I didn't know who to talk to about it, and I was a bit frightened. So I did exactly what worked for me before—nothing.

When Connor was born, I knew that the marriage was over and done with. Although my husband didn't tell me in so many words, his actions spoke loud and clear. My guides, including Poe, tried to help me keep my sanity intact by offering comforting words, but I was devastated. I rationalized the divorce with the idea that maybe we could fall in love again and remarry. It wasn't easy to sign divorce papers when I thought I was still so madly in love with the man that I was divorcing. Connor was two years old and Micaela four.

I was uncertain how I was going to survive with two small kids, no job, no college degree, and a house filled with spirits, one a famous author, another an Irish beauty called Tallie, and Alto, a Native American. My only idea was to wait for the men in the white coats to come and take me away.

But they didn't, so I had to make it work and learn to integrate what I felt at the time was crazy into the reality of the current situation.

"You will write, Kristy," Poe suggested.

"How did that go for you?" I snapped, meanly.

I know that it didn't serve me any good to mistreat my guides, the only people in my life who had never really abandoned me or let me down. It was me who decided to shelve them and go it alone, but I was frustrated and sad.

"Playing dirty, are you now? We know that you are upset and we know that you are hurting right now. I promise—it will get better. And by the way, I didn't write for money, but because I loved to write. The money part was a technicality."

But I wanted things better right then. I wanted my family back together, and I wanted to not hurt so badly.

To make matters even more complicated, both Micaela and Connor were seeing spirits. They were refusing to sleep in their rooms, so we were all camping out in the living room on a large sectional couch. And when their father found out, he had a fit.

"Enough with the ghosts, Kristy. Enough with thinking you can see and talk with them, and you better not get our kids involved or I will…," he sternly commanded, "I will take them away from you."

This time, though, I couldn't ignore it and I wasn't going to allow my now ex-husband to mold my identity. I allowed it once and that about did me in. Plus, I knew that seeing so-called imaginary friends wasn't going to get the kids taken from me. At least I prayed that it wasn't.

So I did what Poe recommended. I wrote. And I found a job that allowed me to write newsletters, web pages, and copy. Just after Connor was born, I had started a company writing personalized Santa Claus, Easter Bunny, and tooth fairy letters. It helped with some money and it helped me to fine-tune my psychic abilities by channeling information for the letters. It would come together. I just didn't know how long it would take. Or how long I could wait.

chapter four

– November 2004 –

Connor was seven and Micaela was ten years old when I
met Chuck on a blind date. After being hurt so badly, it
was odd that I felt so comfortable with Chuck. I joked that
after the first day he came over to my house, I never got rid
of him, and there was a truth to that. I still had wounds and
I was concerned about being hurt again, and yet I wasn't
worried that Chuck would hurt me.

I was going through court proceedings to go back to
my maiden name when Chuck and I met.

"You might as well just change it to Robinett right
now," Chuck said seriously.

"Uh-huh," I grinned. Now that was insanity.

"What?" He innocently looked at me. "You are going
to have to go through this name-change thing soon anyhow."

I checked with my guides, and they nodded that he was right.

It was on that first date that I laid everything out on the table about my abilities and my sixth sense. I didn't, however, tell him who my guides were, even though Poe took full credit for the matchmaking.

I soon learned Chuck snored something fierce, so we normally didn't sleep together in the same bed. He would sleep on the couch with my black cat, Oswald. We were just feet away from one another, as my home was only about 900 square feet. One afternoon we ended up falling asleep together in a nap. As I snuggled against him, images of several past lives together flooded my vision. It was as if someone had put a movie on in front of me and hit fast forward, or rewind, however you want to look at it. I caught blips of pictures, images, words, and even emotions from what I was being shown, but nothing was completely coherent. I woke up, grabbed my notepad, and wrote down everything that I saw. As I was scribbling, Chuck woke, stretched, and just watched. I was determined to get everything on paper and it was apparent without having to communicate it. Once I was finished, I set the notepad on the oak nightstand, snuggled back into his arms, and began to cry.

"What was that all about?" Chuck asked.

"Do you believe in reincarnation?"

"Absolutely," he answered without hesitation.

I leaned on him, looking into his brown eyes that most of the time sparkled with laughter and teasing. This time they were serious.

"You don't?" he asked me.

I thought back to the conversation I'd had with Poe years ago.

"It goes against what I was taught. It goes against my religion. And yet…" I took a deep breath. "And yet there are way too many coincidences, or synchronicities, within my life and others. My dreams and visions from past lifetimes and the information that I receive isn't just from spirits and guides, but from firsthand experiences in other times."

"And so what's this all about?" Chuck pointed to my purple spiral notebook.

"I dreamed…" I shook my head and took another deep breath and began again, "No, not dreamed, I had a vision of several lifetimes that we shared together. Do you know anybody with the last name Butler?"

Chuck let out a small laugh. "Yeah, my mom. My great-grandfather was Arthur Henry Butler and my great-grandmother was Cora Margaret Vaugn."

"Well, somehow, some way, we also had the last name Butler in one of our lifetimes."

"Interesting. What else did you see?"

"A lot, actually." I grabbed the notepad. "We lived in this beautiful city, with a park and water in front of us and cobblestone streets. You were a lawyer who decided to become a politician."

"That doesn't surprise me," he said, lifting his chin in an arrogant motion.

"Yeah, well…!" I smirked and continued sharing my notes with him.

"All the lifetimes blended together, to be honest. So, I'm not sure if Butler was a seventeenth-century lifetime or nineteeth-century lifetime."

Chuck shook his head in confusion.

"From what I can gather, there were two lifetimes that we shared. One revolved around Massachusetts and the Salem Witch trials."

"So you were a witch?"

"Perceived as one, yes," I nodded. "Which makes sense as to why I'm so hesitant at this psychic stuff today."

"I wrote down *Bliss*, with a capital B, and I do know that there is a Mary Parsons-Bliss connected. I am not sure of the connection, though," I sighed in frustration.

"Keep going," Chuck urged. "And was I a lawyer in this lifetime?"

I nodded. "It looks like both of these lifetimes you had something to do with law and politics."

"Let's get dinner," Chuck said, stretching. "And take your notebook."

We got ready and went out to the local diner, sitting in a back booth.

My mind wandered to my meditation where my heritage dated back to Ireland, but I was living with my father and two sisters in Winchester, Massachusetts. In the vision, I lost my mother early on and my father was a farmer and was very well-respected by the Native Americans who didn't live far from the land. He worked hand in hand with them, which frightened many of the white men, yet they respected the relationship. The three of us grew up being very open-minded and with special attachment to nature and spiritualism. We grew to respect the air, the water, and the earth. Because of this, we were looked at as possible witches at the same time the chaos in Salem was happening. We weren't accused of witchcraft, but there were whispers.

The youngest sister chose a man that neither I nor my other sister found particularly handsome, but he had a heart of gold. She would get angry at our continuous teasing and storm off and was very good at stomping her right foot. Her husband owned a hotel near a railroad (I kept hearing a train whistle) or some sort of a station and was quite the entrepreneur. I married an attorney who was strong willed and, although loving, could come across as aggressive. And my other sister married a physician who reminded us most of our dear father. Each of us had children, beautiful homes, and really tame lives, thanks to the respect our father had. He never remarried and was quite fond of his sons-in-law and adored his grandchildren.

"Well, it looks like in this lifetime you were afraid that they may point me out as a witch, so you took our family to North Carolina. I hated it there. No, I detested it there and wanted to come back home, but you did what you had to in order to keep us all safe."

"And in the other lifetime?"

I shook my head. "I'm not sure. I wrote down North and South Carolina, Philadelphia, Civil War, law, and poetry, but I haven't a clue what it means."

"Well, one day we will find out, I'm sure," Chuck said, taking a bite of his pulled pork sandwich. "Maybe now isn't the time," he rationalized.

I never liked leaving things unresolved, but I realized that was all I could do. Until I was gifted another vision and in the dream was told to go to Maryland. I had a sneaking suspicion that Poe would be able to help give the reason why.

chapter five

– June 2007 –

The cottage in Solomon's Island, Maryland, was surrounded by state land on one side and the Chesapeake Bay on the other, and it wasn't at all the vacation that the kids had hoped for. But something, or someone—namely Poe—was pulling me into his world. There wasn't any way for me to explain it to Chuck or the kids that it was because, "Edgar Allan Poe, you know the dead poet, well he told me that we had to drive eight-plus hours to Maryland so that I could walk where he walked, visit his grave and home, and get answers to his death." That wasn't happening.

I needed the vacation, though. I was working a corporate job at the time, knowing that wasn't my future course and that a crystal ball, or a Magic 8 Ball even, would validate the same. So even though we weren't next to an amusement park or in a four-star hotel, this vacation felt right to me.

The cottage, although unappealing to look at from the outside, was quite the quaint designer's dream on the inside. With an open concept, there were two small bedrooms on the first floor, with a second-floor attic as a third bedroom. Chuck and I took the master bedroom, while Micaela and Connor were going to share the bedroom off of the kitchen. Chuck's kids, Cora and Molly, would take the top floor, as I figured their late-night calls to their boyfriends and friends would be less likely to keep us awake if they were up there. But that didn't last a night.

We decided that since the drive was so long, we would get groceries and then just hang around the cottage and rest until morning. We ate dinner, which consisted of grilled hamburgers, and finished cleaning up the dishes. The sun was beginning to set. Chuck was sitting on the red couch watching baseball while I was sitting in a large, cotton pinstriped chair reading when the girls all but flew down the narrow stairway, squealing.

Chuck, like most men, isn't thrilled when his television viewing is interrupted, and this was no exception, as it was the All-Star baseball game.

"I'm pretty sure there is a ghost here," Cora shrieked.

"And why do you say that?" I asked, glancing over at the stairwell to see Poe standing there, grinning from ear to ear.

Molly's eyes were bright and alert. "We heard a whisper and then something moved along the back wall, a shadow. Can you go check?"

Chuck, although frustrated at the moment from being tired from the long drive and just wanting to watch the game, was normally very low-key and laid-back. Nothing much fazed him, including ghosts and spirits. With four kids, he was fine with catching spiders and letting them outside, checking on potential burglars or ghosts, and overall being the family hero. But as Chuck got up to check out the potential spirit, I shooed him back down, as I already knew who the prankster was.

"I'll look. You girls just stay here."

Connor popped out of his room, holding his handheld electronic game. "I'll go with you, Mom."

Both Micaela and Connor had a deeper understanding of the paranormal life, and although I never told them that there wasn't any such thing as ghosts, I didn't make it an everyday conversation or experience.

"It's okay, Con. I'll be just a second. I bet it was just a squirrel on the roof or something."

Connor nodded, but he looked a bit disappointed. He had been the man, little man that is, of the house for so many years before Chuck came on the scene, and sometimes I thought maybe I needed to allow him to be a hero during innocent times. Although I knew this was one of those times, I needed a few minutes alone to talk to Poe.

I climbed the steep staircase into the attic. With each step the maple floors creaked, and my heart began to beat faster and faster. Maybe I was wrong. Maybe it was something other than Poe. Maybe it was a trap. What if a ghost, or worse, a great big spider or a bat jumped out at me? But no, when I got to the top of the stairwell I saw Poe sitting on the full-size bed looking out the window toward the seashore.

"Well, here we are, Edgar. Maryland. I know it isn't your treasured Virginia or Philly, but..."

He turned around and looked at me. "You have a nice family, Kristy."

"Thanks?"

"No, I mean it. Your life is going to change soon. Look for the signs because they will be all around you. Just don't take for granted this quiet time this week."

I sat down next to him on the bed. "So now what, Poe? Why am I here other than to enjoy the quiet?"

"Go to Baltimore. Don't look for anything, just go. You will find it."

He was probably the most enigmatic guide I had, which drove me insane, but I trusted him and it made me wonder if I was either naïve or just insane myself.

"Mom!" Connor called, halfway up the stairway.

"Coming," I got up off the bed and called down the stairway. "I think maybe it was just the wind."

I turned back to Poe. "Don't scare the kids anymore, okay?"

He didn't answer; he just grinned his crooked smile.

Even with my reassurances, the girls decided that they weren't going to stay upstairs, so they lugged their belongings into the spare room and the four kids bunked together. None of them seemed to have a problem with it, so both Chuck and I left it alone.

"What's the plan for tomorrow?" Chuck asked, using the remote to turn the television off.

"Baltimore."

My dreams that night were restless and disjointed, but filled with dark shadows—groups of figures that resembled men all dressed in trench coats and short black hats hid in alleyways and in door stoops, watching me as I walked alone along a narrow cobblestone street. The shadows of the buildings did nothing to protect me and the aura from the streetlights seemed to only leave me feeling exposed. It was only a matter of time before I was taken. There was no escape.

June 1848

I looked down at my clothing to see a blue wool dress and sturdy shoes. A wedding band decorated my left hand, and in my right hand I held a handkerchief with the initials S. B. embroidered on it. I wondered if I had children, yet my soul said I had several.

I could hear footsteps behind me, getting closer, but I feared looking behind me. Instead I carried myself quickly forward. But before I could even attempt a detour, a calming melodic voice whispered in my ear, "Just keep walking, Sara. With me by your side, you will get home safely."

I briefly glanced over my shoulder to see familiar gray eyes meet mine.

"Who are they?" I quietly whimpered.

"They are your government. They are your law enforcers. They are your farmers. And your shop keepers, your politicians, your doctors. They are your ministers. They are..."

I gasped awake and, with my arms flailing, knocked over my eyeglasses I had sitting on the nightstand next to me. While trying to catch them, my glass of water tumbled, pouring onto the wooden floor.

Disturbed by the nightmare and disgusted at making a menace of myself first thing in the morning, I looked over at Chuck to see that my bumbling hadn't stirred him from his sleep.

I wiped down the water with a beach towel that I had packed and quietly made my way into the living room to watch the sunrise. With a blue cotton blanket drawn over my shoulders, I attempted to revisit the vision in a waking, meditative state. But nothing happened. I felt a bit like Samantha in *Bewitched* trying to wiggle my nose in hopes that some magic would happen, but no matter what I did—sat up, laid down, got into a yoga pose—I couldn't capture the vision again. However, I couldn't shake the feeling of being watched and feeling as if I was a lamb going to slaughter, to be sacrificed in order to teach another a lesson.

But why? And by who? I needed a revelation of sorts. I looked around for Alto or Poe, or maybe even Tallie, although she tended to stay away from the drama. There wasn't anybody there but me and the sunshine. Oh, and a cute, little, brown field mouse that had found its way into the house the night before and was camping out in the kitchen. I made a note to myself to see if Chuck could help find it a new home outside.

———————

"I have never been so hot in my entire life," Cora complained, tying her long, brown hair into a ponytail and wiping the back of her neck.

She was right. The six of us were standing in the middle of Baltimore, looking over the harbor, roasting in what had to be low hundred degree temperatures. We grabbed some waters to begin our walking tour.

"First we find Edgar Allan Poe's gravesite," I said to everyone's moans. "Hey, it's history," I reasoned.

"How far?" Micaela asked in a whiny voice, drawing out the two words to sound more like a hundred.

I looked at Chuck to see if he knew, but he only shrugged. "Let's go this way," I said, pointing away from the water. "And I will ask someone if we can't find it," I tried to reassure the group.

We walked and walked and walked, while I began singing the *Sesame Street* theme song, only changing the lyrics to "Can you tell me how to get, how to get to

Westminster Hall?" And yes, I realized it didn't flow quite as well. A man dressed in a suit and looking very professor-like and dignified laughed at my silliness and pointed the way, but he offered a warning that the neighborhood could be rough and to go in quickly and get out quickly. I turned to the kids, who were mortified all the way around, but I impressed upon them how my singing got us directions.

Westminster Hall is a beautiful historic building. It is located at the intersection of Fayette and Greene Streets in downtown Baltimore. The graveyard was established in 1786 by the First Presbyterian Church. Over the next sixty years, the grounds became the final resting place for the important and the who's-who residents of early Baltimore. Of course, one of the most famous residents was writer Edgar Allan Poe, who was buried there in October 1849 following his sudden and mysterious death. In 1852, a church was erected overtop the graveyard, straddling gravestones and burial vaults to create what is now referred to as the catacombs.

No search had to be conducted to find Poe's grave as the monument stood tall near the gate with a stone etching of a raven atop it. Various gifts laid on top and around it to honor the gothic writer. Poe wasn't originally buried there, but was instead buried around the corner in a family plot. In 1875, a local schoolteacher started a "Pennies for Poe" campaign to raise money for a more appropriate monument. Poe was reburied there along with his aunt and mother-in-law, Maria Clemm, and his wife, Virginia.

It is there that visitors continue to leave pennies, flowers, and even alcohol.

Beginning in the 1930s, on Poe's birthday, January 19, an unidentified man known as the Poe Toaster visited the burying ground to make an annual tribute to Poe. Dressed in black with a wide-brimmed hat and white scarf, the shadowy figure would pour himself a glass of cognac and raise a toast to Poe's memory. He would then vanish into the night, leaving three roses in a distinctive arrangement and the unfinished bottle of cognac. The tradition sadly ended in 2009.

Chuck held out pennies to each of the kids. "We should honor him."

I looked at the family gathered around Poe's grave, tempted to make my confession, but I caught a black shadow out of the corner of my eye in the back of the graveyard. Forgetting about the forewarning to be careful, I walked away from the group to see if the shadow was human or spirit. A hand on my back caught me off-guard and I squealed and spun around. Connor's gray eyes looked back at me.

"I saw something, Mom."

"Me too. Let's go see."

We walked through the narrow passage, through various graves. There weren't trees to protect us from the smoldering heat, so we kept dabbing our sweating foreheads. Neither of us saw the shadow again, and there didn't appear to be another human visiting the cemetery. I figured that even ghosts were dying in the heat (pun intended), so we rejoined the family.

The kids whined of hunger, so we made the decision to make our way back toward the harbor. I couldn't get over the fact that I felt a presence watching me, but each time I turned around, I was met with nobody.

"A hitchhiker?" Chuck asked me, after my sixth time turning and looking behind us.

Sometimes when I went to haunted locations, or even just cemeteries, I would pick up a spirit attachment that we lovingly referred to as a hitchhiker. No matter if the cemetery was historic or newer, upon leaving the gates I would always tell the spirits that they must remain and not follow me. And Westminster Hall was no different. The spirits, however, didn't always listen to me.

I shook my head and bit my bottom lip, perplexed. "I'm not quite sure what it is. Connor felt it, too, but I don't *see* anything."

Chuck took my gift all in stride (for the most part). And so far so good, as he hadn't called on the men with the white coats to come and get me.

"Now where?"

"Let's take the water taxi to Fell's Point," I said. "But let's eat first."

I had hoped the kids would be in a better mood after having some food in them, but it seemed to have the opposite effect and the temperatures were only rising. Thankfully the boat ride to Fell's Point offered some relief, as there was a shaded canopy.

Purchased in 1726 and founded in 1763 by William Fell, Fell's Point, a neighborhood in Baltimore, became a shipbuilding and commercial hub. In the late 1700s and early 1800s the harbor area was often riddled with crime and pirates. Today, its cobblestone streets, historic buildings, row houses, and eclectic boutiques were quaint. Once we got off the boat it seemed we all fell in love with the place. It also helped that the temperatures seemed to drop several degrees, making it a bit more bearable.

"What is here, Mom?" Micaela asked me, looking worn from the heat and all the walking.

"Well, there are some cute shops and restaurants. And," I hesitated for a moment, "so is the last place Edgar Allan Poe was ever seen alive."

"Where are you?" I asked Poe in my head. The kids and Chuck had wandered into a souvenir shop and I was trying to take a moment to connect with him in hopes of figuring out why we were even here. *A clue, any clue, would be nice about now, Poe.*

"There, that was the last place I was seen coherent." Poe popped up and pointed to a small bar just down from a historic hotel and a block away from the water.

I gave him a sideways look.

"Everybody I ever loved died. Everybody. From childhood's hour I have not been. As others were, I have not seen. As others saw, I could not awaken. My heart to joy at the same tone. And all I loved, I loved alone."

"Don't get all doom and gloom on me now, Edgar. You might have lost your family, but you were a ladies' man if there ever was one. We call that a player today."

Poe rolled his eyes, but underneath them his usually stern, closed-lip mouth was a grin. He knew that I was right.

"So, can you start at the beginning? Why were you here in Baltimore to begin with? Many say that you got on the wrong train," I egged him on.

"I knew my trains and I knew my directions," Poe huffed, then he shook his head in despair. "I want to see what you get first, before I share anything else with you."

Great. I didn't care for stump-the-psychic games with real people and now even spirits were going to play.

Seeing that he wasn't going to help me, I glowered at him and then closed my eyes. Trying to take myself back to October 3, 1849, I wished there was an easier way rather than remote viewing or astral travel, if only someone had invented time travel of some kind.

But the energy around me seemed to cooperate. The first thing I was shown was Poe slithering through a back alleyway. He looked around him, jittery. Wearing a stained and faded coat, ratty pantaloons, a pair of worn-out shoes, and an old straw hat—all of which was out of character— he stood with his back against the stone wall. Actually, I thought he looked ridiculous.

A man, dressed in a long black coat and black hat, strolled up to Poe from the opposite way that Poe had entered the alleyway.

"This is a bad idea," the man whispered, his eyes darting right and left. "I think I was followed."

Poe began to walk toward a building across from the alleyway.

"Where are you taking me?" the man whispered to Poe.

"Shhh...," Poe responded.

"This isn't how I operate, Poe. Pinkerton was very clear," he chided with a thick Scottish accent.

"You will understand soon enough. We have a deal."

Shrouded only by their coats, the two men slipped into a back door of a large, gray stone building that looked familiar to me, but not in this time.

Pinkerton, I thought. The name sounded familiar. *Could it be that he was referring to Allan Pinkerton of the Pinkerton Detective Agency,* I wondered?

In 1844, Pinkerton worked for Chicago Abolitionist leaders, and his home was a stop on the Underground Railroad. A few years later, he became the very first detective in Chicago. A year later, he met his partner in a Masonic Temple and formed the Pinkerton Detective Agency. It is still in existence today, but known as Pinkerton Consulting & Investigations. I was trying to think back if I remembered Pinkerton visiting Baltimore, but then the history books didn't have everything in them.

It wasn't long afterward that the two men stepped out and slithered through the alleyway.

Poe looked exasperated and shook his head in disgust. "Meet me by the harbor at dusk," he said and walked off toward the local tavern.

"Hey, Mom, look, there's a palm reader. Cora wants to go," Connor said, pulling gently at my purse, waking me from my trance.

"Yes, of course," I smiled, shaking my head of the vision.

For the remainder of our time in Baltimore, I felt exhausted. I wasn't sure what to make of the glimpse from the past that I had been given. The heat certainly wasn't helping anything either. I kept looking around to see if Poe reappeared, but to no avail. He wasn't anywhere in the physical world, or at least around me.

Our trip back to the cottage didn't seem to take long at all. We were all eager to take a shower and curl up in our pajamas. Just as we all got settled in to play a game of cards at the dining room table, we all heard a strange noise. It sounded like typing.

The house had an oak armoire with doors and within it was a computer free for our usage. Internet was dicey, as was the phone signal at the remote location, but I was using it to check in with work every morning. That morning, since we got an early start, I hadn't even bothered. But we had certainly heard the sound of typing.

Molly slowly opened up the armoire doors. "I can hear keys being typed, but I don't see them being typed. No words on the screen either."

"Let's do a séance!" Cora chimed in.

"No!" Micaela cried.

Micaela hated anything to do with the paranormal world. Since I was the ghost magnet, I sometimes think that she hated me, too.

Chuck began clearing off the dining room table. "A séance sounds like fun."

"Yeah, to you," I mumbled under my breath. "This is like work to me. Why don't we just keep playing Uno?"

But despite Micaela's and my own uneasiness with the activity, I reluctantly gave in to my family's peer pressure.

It was already dark outside, so we turned off the lights within the house and lit a couple candles. I said a prayer of protection and we began to call on anyone in the spirit world who wanted to talk to us. Immediately we could hear footsteps in the attic. They started off sounding like one person walking, but as it continued it sounded like several people were.

Micaela put her hands over her head. "I told you this was a bad idea!"

And just as the footsteps stopped upstairs, the typing once again started at the desktop computer.

"Edgar, is that you?" I asked in my mind. I couldn't feel him or any of my other guides and thought maybe Micaela was more psychic than she let on because this was beginning to be a very bad idea.

The energy swirled around us, much like that before a severe lightning storm. Something fell in the kitchen and we all jumped. The footsteps quieted, as did the typing.

I got up out of my chair and everyone looked at me curiously. "I'm checking the computer," I whispered. Tip-toeing over to the armoire, which was only a few feet away, I looked at the screen. There on the screen was a word. Just one.

Brotherhood.

"Anything there?" Cora asked, getting up from her seat.

I hit the button for another screen. "Nope. Nothing. Just like before."

Chuck looked disbelievingly at me. I was a really bad liar.

"Let's just shut this down and go to bed. It has been a long day."

"What are we doing tomorrow?" Connor asked.

"I'm thinking after this exciting and tiring day that we should just chill tomorrow. Let's just go to the beach and then go into town for some ice cream."

When did vacations get to be so exhausting? I thought. *Oh, that's right, when you become an adult with kids.*

As soon as the kids were tucked in, I kissed Chuck good night and crawled into bed with a notebook and pen and poured out the day onto paper. Writing down not only the visions, but also what happened that day and the emotions that I felt. Feeling satisfied that I remembered everything, I again called on Poe to see if he would come through and give me more, but the phone line to the dead was coming up a busy signal.

It stayed off the hook for almost six months, leaving me to research anything to do with Edgar Allan Poe and what the Brotherhood connection was. When he finally came through, he told me that I would eventually need to go to Asheville, North Carolina. I was beginning to think that he was part of some tourist division and just wanted me to travel.

chapter six

– June 2010 –

I knew that I had to go to Asheville, but I didn't really understand why. Poe merely told me to find a lodging house that would be open to me having a séance there. I had been doing séances for several years, mostly during October for Halloween-type events, although the séances I conducted weren't parlor tricks and fun, but instead a means to connect guests with the other side. I hadn't a clue how I was going to put my feelers out from Michigan and find a warm reception. So on New Year's Eve 2009, I began looking for a bed and breakfast. I simply put keywords into Google—*Bed and Breakfast* and *Asheville*.

I pulled up three prospects. One in particular looked riveting, except the website was down. There was only the static page with its name; The Reynolds Mansion, Previously the Old Reynolds Mansion; a picture of the inn; COMING SOON; and a phone number. It had no opening date, but I marked it down for my assistant Donna to call anyhow. It was the end of the first week of January when Donna phoned me, sounding breathless and excited.

"Kristy, you have to call Billy as soon as possible. He is the owner of the Reynolds Mansion in Asheville, and I think this is perfect for you. He wasn't even afraid when I told him you were a psychic." Donna laughed. "How excited is the owner to have you? Too excited! It was such a fun conversation!"

"Wait, slow down, Donna." I laughed into the phone.

Without skipping a beat, she continued, "The mansion isn't open for business until March. It has been closed for four years, and he says if you contact him in March, he will be available to give you any date you want. The dining table (there is only one) holds exactly twenty people. He will not have rates available until February," Donna breathlessly finished and took a deep and happy sigh.

Donna is not a psychic but she is quite gifted with a sense of knowing, and I always trusted her opinions, so if she said I needed to call Billy, I needed to call Billy.

So after catching up about the previous holiday, we hung up and I dialed the North Carolina phone number only to receive a voicemail. I left a brief message about needing to speak to Billy about an event in the summertime, and before I hung up my other line was ringing from the same number.

"Thanks so much for calling me back," I said when I answered.

"No, thank you for calling us, Kristy," Billy said, his slow, southern drawl wooing me.

I explained to him that I was looking for a place that had a haunted history to hold an event at. No, I had never been to Asheville, but I felt as if I was being called there to do this and that I didn't know why. All right, it wasn't all me. I knew that Poe was pushing me to go to Asheville, but I didn't know why. What I found ironic, however, was that the last name Poe uttered before his passing was one and the same—Reynolds.

"I promise I'm not crazy," I giggled into the phone. "Wait, probably all crazy people say that!"

Billy chuckled. "If you only knew how much this all makes sense to me, Kristy."

We spoke for almost an hour, both in awe, but not surprised, at the serendipitous encounter. Billy and his partner Michael always wanted to own a B & B. Well, I take that back, Billy always wanted a B & B and in good partnerships you support your partner's passion. In youth, Billy said he wanted to own a large plantation-type home and when he and Michael looked around Asheville, they fell in love with the Reynolds Mansion even though it was in disarray.

"Oh, Kristy, this place was a mess. A normal person would've thought I was nuts to have fallen in love with it, but I saw the diamond in the rough. And after we pulled back the ivy and took down the trees, the mansion began to shine back to its original glory. We are nowhere near done with renovations, but we are hoping to open in March or

April, so a June event will work just fine. And, I sort of knew you were going to call me."

I was confused. I mean I knew that Donna had called, but the way that he said it had a deeper meaning.

"What do you mean, Billy?" I curiously asked.

"Well, you see, Michael and I have a friend in Chicago who is psychically gifted, and we sort of tested her." Billy mischievously laughed. "We met with her over dinner and put several photographs, face down, and asked her which she thought was best for us. One by one, she offered us her impressions and then flipped the photographs over. Now, realize that the photos of this mansion didn't look at all appealing. And some of the photos were homes that were not for sale at all. She immediately pulled out the photo of the Reynolds Mansion and said that there was good energy here and that others would see it, too. And although it is haunted, we'd never feel threatened here, but that the hauntings would draw people to it. So, you see, I knew you would be calling, I just didn't know it would be so soon!"

I expressed my concern that I couldn't draw a crowd to the event, but Billy put my mind at ease by giving me the old adage that if I build it, they will come. And so I simply began advertising a Supernatural Weekend.

Spend the weekend (June 11th and June 12th) with the supernatural at the Reynolds Mansion in Asheville, North Carolina. Experience a Séance, Readings with Psychic Medium Kristy Robinett, and a Paranormal Investigation. Spend the night in this very haunted mansion, which dates back to 1847, and was once used as a sanitarium. The Reynolds Mansion is newly owned and boasts three floors, rooms with hot tubs, two cottages, and four acres of haunted history. Witness firsthand how renovations can stir up ghostly activity.

Chuck and I set out on our journey to North Carolina in the early morning of June 10. We knew that it would be a long drive, over nine hours, but the excitement about the destination made it all worth it.

I had a difficult time going through the mountains in Tennessee and at one point begged Chuck to get off at the nearest exit so that I could get ill. As soon as we pulled into the McDonald's, it began to pour to the point you couldn't see the windy road in front of you. As soon as I got back in the car, less than ten minutes later, the rain had stopped and the sun had come out to dry the roads with its southern rays. I don't believe in coincidences and took this as a sign of protection and blessing.

The mansion was an ominous sight even in the daylight, but one that made me excited and giddy. I felt as if this was destiny; a trip that had to be completed in order for me to put visions of a past life to rest, or at least connect more dots. Poe had already told me to let go of any expectations and just enjoy North Carolina with fresh eyes. But I felt that couldn't be done until I met the demons from that past and handed the keys over to them for a new tenant. It was breathtaking how the southern mansion was returned to her original glory. She glowed from the attention and the love.

"Let me take you on a tour," Billy urged, welcoming us with a hug and handing us a glass of cold lemonade as if we were long-lost friends.

The Reynolds Mansion was built in 1847 and is listed on the National Register of Historic Places. One of the few remaining pre-Civil War homes, the mansion sits on several acres with exceptional views of Reynolds Mountain. With wraparound porches, twelve fireplaces, and exquisite furnishings, the warmth and Southern hospitality is felt immediately when you pull up to the three-story mansion. Once inside, the comforts continue with music playing, reminiscent of the 1940s, and an elaborate, wide, winding staircase gracing the entrance. Above the staircase, nostalgic of the movie *Gone with the Wind,* hangs a portrait of Scarlett O'Hara.

Just on cue, we were greeted by two adorable bulldogs named Rhett and Scarlett who decided against the tour and instead laid in the sun on the steps. Billy took us to the second floor, where he explained that each floor had a Keurig® machine for coffee and tea, cold drinks, and fat pills—muffins, cookies, etc. I wasn't sure we were ever going to leave. He continued to name each room in the mansion one-by-one, which were named after treasured relatives of Billy's and Michael's.

I had reserved Inez's room. It was a small room on the third floor with a happy vibe. In the colors of coral, red, and black, the room just sang with whimsy. As we made our way to the top floor with our luggage, Billy asked me over and over if this was the room I was supposed to have, not the room that I wanted. I saw Poe standing behind Billy, but he gave no indication that it mattered, so I told him that it was just fine.

Before Billy could leave us to unpack, I was pulled to the room across the hall, where I noticed a young lady sitting in the chair. Billy carefully watched me as I stepped around him and wandered into the room named Maggie.

"Billy, have there been any sightings of a young woman in this room?"

Billy was quick to explain that the third floor was probably the most active for paranormal activity. "The Reynolds Mansion actually has no history of tragic death, and unlike many homes from this era, it was never raided or ransacked during the Civil War. But…" He squinted while looking at me. "There was a significant renovation at the end of the last century by Nathaniel Augustus Reynolds. That was when they raised the ceiling and added this third floor. Oddly enough, it is this third floor where the majority of the ghostly activity seems to happen." He gave me a slightly cockeyed look. "You might have seen the ghost of Annie Lee. She's sometimes seen as young, and sometimes old, but we think she is one and the same."

I peeked back into the room and the spirit still sat there, unbeknownst of my presence. Her thick, dark brown hair, with a slight curl, hung over her shoulders. With her thin build and prominent cheekbones, she looked to be maybe about twenty years of age. She was dressed in a cotton floral dress and held a knitting needle and yarn in her lap, lost in her own thoughts. Every so often she would look up and out the window at the expansive yard, as if patiently awaiting someone's arrival.

"It was soon after Michael and I purchased the mansion and were doing renovations when a bride and her mom came to meet with me about having a wedding shower here," Billy said, peeking around me every so often to see if he could see what I did. "I didn't hear them come in, and they took me by surprise. They looked a bit upset with me and went on to explain that they had been waiting awhile. I asked them why they didn't ring the bell and they said that they didn't have to, a young girl let them into the house and ran off when they asked if she would let me know they had arrived. I was obviously puzzled and didn't know what to say other than shake my head. I said that nobody else was here but Michael and myself, and I thought they were going to run for the hills and look for another location to have their event."

"And you think that might have been Annie Lee?"

Billy nodded. "Here." Billy grabbed my hand and led me to a glass cabinet in the hallway. "See this hairpin?"

Several odd treasures lay in the case, but he pointed specifically to a rusty hairpin. "One day this just appeared."

"What do you mean it just appeared?" I asked, confused.

"I had made the bed in Maggie's room, and a couple hours later went in the room to find this lying on the middle of the bed. Nobody had been here, Kristy. It just appeared."

I had cases where such paranormal obscurity had happened, but it was rare. I had objects disappear more than appear. It made me wonder if the Reynolds Mansion had a portal of some sort between times. Maybe this is why Poe wanted me here. I *had* asked for time travel.

As we unpacked, I continued to feel pulled to Maggie's room. Although the lady remained, the spirit didn't acknowledge me. This time she sat in the armchair, reading next to the window that looked out to the front of the home.

We decided to go to dinner, and after changing out of our travel clothes met up with Billy in the library. As Billy showed Chuck a map of the area, I let out a gasp.

"Billy, are you a fan of *Dark Shadows*?" I asked, referring to a portrait of Barnabas Collins, or at least the actor who played Barnabas in one of my very favorite television shows.

"Why, yes," he blushed. "I know that it doesn't quite fit in with the classic style of the home, but I love *Dark Shadows.*"

"Me too!" I squealed, while Chuck rolled his eyes and laughed.

I saw Poe sitting in a leather wing-back chair, grinning in delight. I believe that Billy and I were meant to meet, thanks to Poe.

"Let me show you this," Billy grabbed my hand and again led us to the second floor, where for some reason I hadn't even seen the horror movie posters hanging in the hallway.

The house was very much like a personal museum with paintings of Michael's and Billy's families, old photos of the Reynolds Mansion and their family, antiques that each had a story, and just plain loved objects.

"This," Billy pointed at an object in another glass case, "is an authentic vampire hunting kit. Stake, holy water, Bible, and even a coffin key. This is the real deal."

I gawked.

"Oh good, so if we are attacked by vampires, we are safe?" Chuck asked teasingly.

Billy and I nodded in unison and then laughed.

"Are you sure you don't want to move to the first floor, Kristy? I think Lila's room would gift you much more sleep."

Thinking that sleep was probably a good idea, we took Billy up on his proposal and switched rooms to a gorgeous first-floor room with sixteen-foot ceilings, a crystal chandler, a queen bed, and a beautiful gas fireplace. It looked very elegant. Once settled, we headed off to dinner.

Chuck and I decided to venture into downtown Asheville to find a bite to eat. Taking in the eccentric community that seemed to boast a hippie feel from a bygone decade, we drank in the mountain air, ate organic pizza, and enjoyed some southern sweet tea. Evening caught up with us quickly, and we decided to rest and enjoy the mansion.

Using the facilities in our new room, I immediately felt the spirit of an older man who smelled of strong cologne. Chuck was unaware of what I had seen and rested in the room while I socialized on the front porch. When I checked on him an hour or so later, he told me that he saw a gray figure of a man in the corner of the room. As the figure moved into the chandelier's light, his clothes turned to color. He then smelled a strong smell of men's cologne. Since he rarely sees spirits, he was pretty excited and loved the validation when I shared my experience along with what Billy had told me.

"Oh, that would be Mr. Reynolds," Billy validated. "He died in that room."

I laughed and questioned him on if the room move was a good idea or not. Then I wondered if perhaps the cologne smell was to disguise the scent of death. Was it going to be a busy night?

Billy and Michael, along with other guests, sat on the front porch marveling at the magic the fireflies offered when Billy gave us a brief history lesson of our home away from home for the next couple days. The Reynolds Mansion's website filled in the rest of the history.

Colonel Daniel Reynolds built the imposing brick home on a knoll of Reynolds Mountain in 1847, where he and his wife, Susan Adelia Baird, had ten children, five boys and five girls. The land, a total of 1,500 acres, was a gift from Susan's father, Isreal Baird.

Daniel Reynolds passed away in 1878, and his son, William Taswell Reynolds, inherited the home known as the Reynolds House, along with 140 acres that remained with the estate. In 1880, William Taswell married Mamie Spears and they had four children, including Robert Rice Reynolds, who would become a US Senator in the 1930s.

In 1890, William Taswell sold the house and land to his younger brother, Natt Augustus Reynolds. Two years later, William passed away at the age of forty-two. Ten years after that, Mamie Spears Reynolds married Natt Augustus Reynolds. It wasn't necessarily out of love, Billy was quick to point out, it was more convenience and to keep the family living within the highly acclaimed status.

In the early 1930s, Natt and Mamie moved back to the house and helped raise two of Senator Robert Reynolds's children by his first wife, Frances. Frances had died of typhoid fever when the children, Frances and Robert Rice Reynolds II, were less than three years old.

Senator Reynolds, known as "Our Bob," took residence at the Reynolds House while serving as a US Senator from North Carolina. His fifth wife was Evelyn Washington McLean who was the owner of the famous Hope Diamond.

"In the den, we have a replica of that Hope Diamond," Billy smiled, "and boy does that have a story in itself. Today, the diamond is displayed at the Smithsonian in Washington, DC, but it is said that it has a curse upon it and may even be haunted—so it's there for safekeeping."

Mamie Spears Reynolds died in the 1940s and Natt's daughter, Adelene Reynolds Hall, came to live in the mansion with her father. She was married to Lawrence Hall and they had three children, Natt, Margaret, and Annie. They ran the Hall Coal Yard and the house was referred to as the Hall house at that time.

Natt "Gus" Reynolds died in the 1950s and left the house to Adelene. She in turn left it to her daughters, Annie and Margaret. The house was sold at least two more times before Fred and Helen Faber bought it in 1970. They rebuilt and restored the home, updating the kitchen but trying not to change any more than was necessary. They opened it as a B & B in 1972, calling it the "Old Reynolds Mansion."

"Not much has changed since 1847, except for adding more bathrooms," Michael shared.

On September 13, 1984, the Reynolds Mansion was listed on the National Register of Historic Places and was placed in a protected status. Fewer than ten brick houses survived the Civil War, and the Reynolds Mansion is one of them.

"When Fred died in 2003, Helen tried to keep it up, but it was just too much work for her. After thirty years of loving this home, this," Billy gestured lovingly to the mansion, "became ours."

As I enjoyed the variance of drawls, I noticed that one of the porch lights flickered as certain people were mentioned. I pointed it out, but I was met with smirks and smiles until the others witnessed it. After that no matter how much we tried to debunk and imitate, we could not reproduce it. I welcomed the beginning of a supernatural weekend.

Exhausted from the drive and knowing that we had a big weekend ahead, Chuck and I went to bed as early as we could, but it wasn't too long after that I was awakened.

At 1:20 a.m., I woke up to find the spirit of a man standing at the foot of our bed. Dressed in tails and holding a black top hat, the spirit glared at me and explained that he was not happy at all that the den was locked. I blinked and he still stood there waiting for me to answer. Not knowing what to do, my first instinct was to run to the en suite bathroom and turn the light on. When I turned around, he was gone. Shaking my head as if perhaps the exhaustion of the drive had made my head fuzzy, I left the light on in the bathroom, but I closed the door without latching it in hopes it would calm me.

I crawled back into the high bed and closed my eyes for a moment only to be bathed in light. Snapping open my eyes, I saw the bathroom door had been flung wide open. The bathroom light that I had turned on in order to feel comforted was instead blinding me. I nudged Chuck, who previously told me to wake him if I needed him.

"What?" he scowled.

"There was a ghost of a man at the foot of the bed," I responded, looking around wondering where he had gone.

"What time is it?"

"One-twenty."

Chuck moaned. "Turn the light on in the bathroom then."

Light normally gives me a feeling of safety. Although I didn't feel threatened in the least, I also didn't quite like sleeping with an angry spirit next to me who knew I could communicate with him.

"I did and the door opened up," I whined like a little girl.

"Put a shoe inside the bathroom, against the door and a shoe outside the door and go to sleep," Chuck mumbled and lovingly patted me on the arm.

I got up, looked around the large room, and took my husband's suggestion with the shoes. Then, I laid back down, feeling somewhat satisfied.

It wasn't long that after that I fell asleep and woke up again to a spirit of a lady. She sat on the end of the bed, stroking my right hand. She told me that she had died and she had been set on a "silly table that made her feel dizzy." She motioned to me like a teeter-totter and I about vomited when I realized that she was telling me she had been embalmed. I closed my eyes and wished her away and it worked, because I awoke to the smell of breakfast cooking and daylight peeking in through the blinds.

Breakfast was promptly at 9:00 in the morning in the dining room. I pulled myself out of one of the most comfortable beds that I had ever slept on to take a quick shower and dress and wait for Chuck to do the same. Before going to the bathroom, I glanced over at my necklace on my nightstand, which laid next to the alarm clock, and contemplated putting it on. Thinking that was silly as I always put my necklace on after the shower, I shook my head and thought perhaps the mountain air was getting to me. After my shower, I put my earrings in and walked over to the table to grab my necklace only to find it wasn't there. And the alarm clock was blank. I inquired to Chuck, who gruffly asked me why he would take my necklace and then marched into the shower. I unplugged the alarm clock and plugged it in again. Nothing. I took it to another plug and plugged it in. Nothing. So, I took it back, plugged it into its original outlet, and went to visit Billy. I explained my predicament, and he assured me that he would find my necklace. I returned to our room and, just as I opened the bedroom door, Chuck held my necklace up. He showed me the odd place where he found it in the bathroom—inside of a glass dish where I know for a fact I never placed it—and the alarm clock was glowing its proper time. Cue the *Twilight Zone* music.

As we sat for breakfast, I reassured Billy that all was okay now and he just smiled as we ate our blueberry salad and homemade biscuits along with something he called eggs in a basket. Each plate was more delicious than the one before.

Friday morning came all too soon with a paranormally active nighttime, but once again the adrenaline of the weekend took hold and thoughts of slumber were pushed far from my droopy lids, even though a nap sounded like heaven. With a morning of television interviews, sessions with clients, and lunch with a grade school friend who had moved to North Carolina, I knew a nap wouldn't happen anytime soon. And then Chuck and I were also telling and re-telling our paranormal tales that seemed to continue on in the morning.

Chuck cherishes his baseball hats. He has hundreds and makes sure to match them to his daily outfit, along with his shoes. It is odd to me, but similar to how a woman chooses her jewelry. And because I know that if there is a hair on his hat, he will go nuts, I also know not to touch them. It seemed that he had placed his Chicago Red Sox hat on the fireplace mantel in our bedroom. As I was running around that morning searching for my lost mother of pearl necklace, Chuck was trying to figure out why his hat was mashed in.

"Did you touch my hat?" Chuck inquired. "Did you perhaps sit on my hat?" He asked again in awe, holding up the caved-in cap.

"Right," I answered in a sarcastic tone, knowing what my fate would be if I had done anything of the kind.

"I found my hat, there." He pointed to the only chair in the room without a piece of luggage on. "But I had left it on the fireplace mantel. That darn spirit moved and then sat on my hat!" he spat.

Chuck decided that perhaps Mr. Reynolds wasn't a Chicago Red Sox fan at all, but more than likely a Cubs fan and had sat on his hat. And Chuck was angry.

After the morning's work, I was ready for a much-needed nap. My sleep was filled with more wildly vivid dreams of centuries past that intertwined with Poe, the Reynoldses, and my own past life, yet none of it was cohesive. Chuck had been napping on the back porch, but must've sensed that I, too, was awake and joined me in the dining room for a soft drink and a snack. I had all but lost track of my Native American guide Alto. I could almost always sense him around me, but ever since reaching the

North Carolina mountains, it was as if he'd disappeared. And while Poe was around, he wasn't being helpful at all. It was in the dining room where I found Poe sitting on the piano bench that sat in the corner, staring up at a portrait of a beautiful lady that was hung above one of the many fireplaces in the mansion.

Billy came out of the kitchen to ask if we needed anything, wiping his brow. He was a hard worker—that much was obvious. He barely had a staff and I was worried he was doing too much himself. I could see Michael with the dogs outside working on the pool. They were a great team and I melted every time I watched the two of them look at one another, as even their glances were filled with a depth of love that most people never witnessed or received.

"Mind if I take a break here with you?" Billy asked, pouring himself a sweet tea and sitting down at the table.

"Not at all," Chuck said. Adding, "It is your home, Billy!"

Billy shook his head. "I want it to be everyone's home who enters."

"Who's that, Billy?" I asked, pointing to the portrait that Poe continued to stare up at.

"That's Felicity. Do you have a moment to hear the story?"

Chuck and I both smiled and nodded. Billy was a natural storyteller, and once he started, we were pulled in to the tale.

"Now, I didn't know anything about this lovely lady when I first saw her in an antique store in Florida, but

I knew that I wanted her immediately. However, the price tag was steep and there was a sign that said that the price would triple if you tried to negotiate.

"Michael and I went back to the car, and I felt dejected. Something told me to go back in there. Michael warned me again about the sign as I left him in the car, and I waved him off. So I went back into the shop and stared up at the dark-haired beauty. I knew that at her pretty little price, almost $3,000," he whispered, as if quieting the fact that he didn't want her to know she wasn't worth that, "I couldn't afford her. The owner came over and said that I looked like I was in love. I told him that I was, and that this was all I wanted for my upcoming birthday gift, but not at that price. He said his wife would probably kill him, but he knocked the price down to a song, less than $1,000. When I walked out of the shop with the painting wrapped and under my arms, I thought Michael was going to be sick."

We all laughed at the image.

"What I didn't realize, however, was that this Cajun beauty was trouble."

"How so?" I asked curiously, looking from the painting and back to Poe.

Billy continued, "Not long after getting her into our then home, paranormal activity began happening. We would hear footsteps when nobody was there. I swore one time I even heard a woman cry. And then there were the kitchen incidents. Michael kept asking me why I kept leaving all of the cupboards and drawers open in the kitchen. I didn't know what he meant until it happened to me. I woke up and went to the kitchen to see every single cupboard and every single drawer open. We moved to another state, and once again hung her up. This time when we got home from work, the plumbing underneath the sink was disconnected and our home was flooded."

Chuck and I sat with our mouths open. "And you think she did it?" Chuck asked.

"Yes. There was no other explanation."

"And here, Billy? Has anything happened here?"

"Oh, lots, but I don't think it's Felicity. I think that someway, somehow, Felicity was helping us find our home. She originally lived in a plantation house in Louisiana. This to her feels like home," Billy said. "The picture of her home, Chretien Point Plantation, is in, well, it's ironically in Maggie's room."

The Ghost Hunter's Guide to New Orleans tells the story of Chretien Point Plantation. The plantation is located in Sunset, Louisiana, fourteen miles north of Lafayette, Louisiana. The Chretien and Neda families were friends and business partners, who also had close ties to the famous pirate, Jean Lafitte. Although an unlikely couple, Hypolite Chretien, a portly man, and Felicité Neda (spelled today as Felicity), beautiful, passionate, and feisty for the time period, fell in love and married. They first built a small and modest home on the family land, but a couple years later, as business continued to escalate and a certain status had to be kept, they built a grand plantation home on the 640 secluded acres on the banks of the Bayou Bourbeau. There, Felicité had three children, two boys and a girl.

Felicité and Hypolite were often found quarreling, but nobody could deny their love. One of the major arguments surrounded the family treasures. The business was successful, from both legal and illegal dealings, and Felicité wanted a larger part of the day-to-day operations. Smugglers were welcomed into their home because they provided a means of avoiding heavy taxes on imported items coming in through New Orleans. The Chretiens befriended these shady merchants, offered them food and drink, and allowed them to use the land for the distribution of their contraband, which included merchandise, gold, silver, and even slaves. Hypolite was quite aware that what he was doing was dangerous dealings, and although he gave enough work to Felicité to keep busy, it wasn't enough for his spunky wife. But it was when Hypolite took their family treasures of gold, silver, and jewelry and had a devoted slave bury it deep within a grove of trees on the cotton plantation under a moonlit sky that Felicité became upset. Despite begging from Felicité, Hypolite refused to divulge the location of the treasure.

In 1838, Felicité and Hypolite lost their infant son to yellow fever. A year later, Hypolite himself passed away, leaving Felicité with two children, 500 slaves, and acres of a plantation to care for, never revealing where he hid the family treasure.

Despite the lost riches, the plantation was extremely well off and everyone around knew it. Hypolite was also a big talker with enough liquor in him, and although Jean

Lafitte was a trusted friend despite being a pirate, his men were not.

Felicité was as unconventional as could be, wearing her treasured and expensive jewels even for day-to-day functions. So upon the news that Hypolite was dead and Felicité was alone, it only made sense that the pirates would try to take advantage of the situation. One night Felicité awakened to a commotion outside. She looked through the bedroom window to see several pirates digging and another coming up her front steps. She ran downstairs, opened the front door, took a gun, and shot him. The shot echoed in the night. The remaining pirates fled while the slaves assisted in burying the dead man in an unmarked grave. It is rumored that the blood could never be washed off the steps and remains even today, along with his spirit.

Billy shared with us that soon after the killing, Felicité took on boarders, including one young man who was a painter. He asked if he could paint her portrait and Felicité agreed. She would sneak away to a back house where she would spend hours allowing this handsome stranger to paint her. Felicité and the painter fell in love, or at least he fell in love with the sassy Cajun. Although she was a rebel, she didn't want to mar her and her children's good name.

It was a faithful slave on her way back from town who alerted Felicité that soldiers were on the way. Felicité, always a quick thinker, directed her staff to kill the poultry and make a huge feast. Setting the table with an array of foods and wine from her cellars, she hoped that her home would be spared. Felicité met the general at the gates to her property and, with a smile, handed him the keys to her home. Skeptical and assuming that it was a setup and she was hiding opposing soldiers, the general directed his men to thoroughly search the property. When no other soldiers were found, the men gorged on the prepared feast. Although Felicité's intentions were smart, it backfired and instead of the men being fed and happy, they were fed and drunk and began burning down the slave quarters and other outbuildings on the property, including the slave hospital, slave church, and barns. They spared the mansion, but they pillaged the furnishings and sent away her slaves with threats that if they didn't leave they would be shot. Without any slaves to continue the plantation, Felicité took her two children and moved to New Orleans.

"A few years later, Felicité passed away and the land and mansion were passed down to her children. In 1863, the plantation was almost destroyed again when it became the scene of the Battle of Little Crow Bayou, and," Billy pointed, "this is one of only three paintings of Felicity that miraculously survived that fire. It was stored in one of the outbuildings where the painter was still staying, mourning the loss of his lover. When he went back in, everything was burned, but she was still intact. You can still see a slight burn mark in the corner."

I didn't know why I felt so drawn to her, and I wondered even more so why Poe was acting like he himself just saw a ghost.

"An interesting fact about the Chretien Point Plantation is that the stairs in their home were replicated for

Gone with the Wind, along with the scene where Scarlett shoots the Union soldier, much like Felicity's own experience on the plantation stairwell. I didn't even know that when I purchased her," Billy said.

After our chat, Billy went back to work and I prepared for the night's séance that was to take place in the dining room. Participants showed up to the nighttime event, sat around the polished table, and were given instructions on what to expect. Fingertips gently placed on the table, forming a circle for protection—the séance began.

I never require validation throughout a séance. I offer the spirits to voice who they are, who they may be for, and what messages they would like to share. Validation in a séance often breaks my concentration (which is different than a regular reading or even a gallery reading) because I offer the spirits, sometimes in the hundreds, their time. It can sometimes be like visiting a kindergarten classroom and making out blips of information from all of the excited kids. It isn't easy. I always close off a séance if I feel something negative is coming through, as I only allow spirits of the higher vibration and white light to come through and anything else to stay away. Well, I didn't get a negative energy, but a very persistent spirit who was blocking anybody else from coming through…Felicité.

She stood next to me, looking much like her portrait that hung only a few feet away. She said she was misunderstood and was referred to as a spirited woman of the nineteenth century. Of that she didn't deny, but she was upset that her reputation may have been overdramatized.

It wasn't that Billy or Michael misspoke of anything in the least, and she was very happy that she was held in such high regard by both of them. She even felt as if the home, the Reynolds Mansion, felt more like the plantation in which she had previously lived. No, it was more that she valued honesty and truths and something in her past wasn't being told truthfully, mainly being that she didn't up and leave her homestead willingly. The Chretien family was going to oust her for having a romance. Her eyes grew clouded. She reiterated how much she prided herself on keeping the plantation home going.

Just as I thought she might leave to unlock the door to the other side for the very patient participants, she eyed Poe sitting in the corner. Their eyes locked in recognition, and they both smiled.

"Have you told her about Reynolds?" Felicité asked Poe.

He shook his head and put his finger up to his lips, asking for her silence.

And then they were gone. The séance continued with knocks, footsteps, and noises, along with messages from loved ones for those around the table.

Afterward my brain felt numb, and although I was eager to ask Poe what Felicity meant and what their relationship was, I just wanted to go to bed. Just then, the B & B's phone rang, making us all jump.

"It's after midnight," Billy commented, in an annoyed manner, but he answered it.

I looked on curiously as he gave directions.

"It's what sounds like two young girls. They weren't aware of your event, but they were looking for a haunted location. I am putting them in Maggie's room," he chuckled.

The irony was a couple never showed up for that night, and although both Billy and I continued to call them, we never received an answer.

"Everything happens for a reason, Kristy," Billy said drowsily and went to the office to await the nighttime guests.

I finished saying goodbyes and good nights, and barely got into my nightclothes before I was dead to the world. I woke up again to the smell of freshly brewed coffee and a thick fog that covered the grounds.

Before breakfast, I took a few minutes to walk the grounds. The morning fog enveloped my legs, making me look as if I was an apparition myself. I sensed a familiar spirit walking next to me. I didn't have to check first to see if it was in fact him, I began without any small talk.

"Who is Felicity to you? Another one on your long list of lost loves?"

I heard him chuckle, the laugh resonating within my mind, but he didn't answer right away. Walking over to a wooden swing that hung from a large oak tree, I sat down and gently kicked my legs.

"And who is Reynolds? Is there any connection to Daniel Reynolds who built this mansion?"

Poe leaned against the tree and sighed. Putting his hand on his head as if he had a headache, he began, "I did know Felicity, but she wasn't a love, although I doted on her so. I met her just once as she was on business in New Orleans, and she stated that she was an admirer of my work. I had taken a trip to meet with a literary magazine and lecture. It was her story that influenced my award-winning short story *The Gold-Bug*."

"And Reynolds? Is the last word you spoke any connection to this?" I pointed to the southern plantation.

"Not Daniel himself, but part of his lineage, yes." Poe took his hand away from his head and placed it to his side. He raised the collar on his coat, which was always an indicator that he was done talking to me, but I needed more answers.

"Care to continue?" I dared.

He shook his head. "No, not yet, Kristy. It isn't time. Oh, the past, it is like a pebble in my shoe," Poe squawked.

I swung higher on the swing, pumping my legs harder and harder. "Dammit, Poe, I am not one of your readers who needs or even wants your cryptograms." When I slowed my swinging I noticed that he was gone. He never did like criticism. I feared that I had ticked him off by not playing his game.

———

"Why don't you stay for another couple days?" Billy pleaded, giving me a hug on the back porch. "It will give you an opportunity to just rest."

The night before the séance there was a ghost investigation. It had been fun and active. The group that came out to investigate was like long-lost friends, and I wondered if it was perhaps the southern hospitality everyone talks about.

The girls who came the night before had many experiences in Maggie's room that left them tired, but also excited. The doorknob jiggled several times as if someone was trying to come into the room, which Billy confirmed was a constant complaint and had the same thing happen on his and Michael's own suite. During the investigation, we heard whispers, heard a dog bark even though Rhett and Scarlett were sound asleep, and several of us were touched, a feeling that can be unsettling. There were extreme temperature changes, and several sensed someone nearby.

"No, we really have to go, even though I don't want to," I said, hugging Billy back.

We weren't heading home. We had scheduled a couple of days in Myrtle Beach to do just what Billy suggested, rest, but this time at the oceanfront.

As Chuck drove the car down the windy road toward the freeway, I felt a bit unsettled and incomplete. I had hoped for more, but I thought maybe I was being too hard on myself and had too high of expectations for something I should have had no expectations. It had nothing to do with the events at the mansion, but more figuring out Poe's puzzle. To make matters more curious, the mysteries seemed to become more entangled rather than solved. I also hadn't seen nor heard from my main guide Alto since we entered North Carolina. It was like I lost him en route. He was my main vein for business and since getting to the Reynolds Mansion I hadn't received one client order when I checked my e-mail, and I was concerned. Not only concerned about Alto, but about my bank account.

The first night in Myrtle Beach made me wish the kids were with us. The hotel and beaches were filled with families and instead of enjoying our time as a couple, I wanted to send an airplane ticket to them for the next flight. If Chuck was expecting any sort of romance from this trip, I am sure he was sorely disappointed.

With my melancholy mood and the hotel room that had two full beds, me in one and Chuck in the other, I got the laptop out and started researching how far Charleston was from where we were. I found it was a little more than an hour away, albeit the opposite direction from home. But there was a pull that I couldn't ignore any longer, and I had an inkling who was tugging.

We had taken the kids to Myrtle Beach a few years before, so seeing that was familiar territory. I had made the hotel reservations, and yet something was still telling me to go to Charleston. When I had called and mentioned it to my girlfriend, she said she didn't care much for Charleston, and it left me feeling confused all over again.

Chuck was always good for spontaneity, me not so much, so when I decide to change the rules smack dab in the middle of the game, he knows to listen.

"Let's go to Charleston."

There, I had said it. It was like a weight had lifted and a feeling of contentment took over. I looked over at Poe, who was standing, staring out the hotel room window at the storm clouds rolling in. He turned around, offered me a wink, and went back to his pondering.

"I know you hate tours and all, but I would like to do a history tour and a ghost tour."

Chuck groaned and tossed his fantasy baseball magazine down on the bed and looked at me sideways. "Why? It's like a surgeon on vacation going to do surgery just for the fun of it."

Point taken.

"I am not quite sure how to explain it…"

Chuck pretended as if I shot him and lay back on the bed, holding his chest.

"I know…so unusual. Can you just trust me on this? Just one night. And I won't purposefully choose a haunted hotel, okay? You'll have fun! I swear." I was telepathically telling Poe that he better make this worth all of our whiles. "I don't want a wild goose chase," I uttered under my breath to Poe.

Chuck groaned again, sat back up on the bed, grabbed his magazine, and began to read. Or he was just simply ignoring me?

I still hadn't divulged to Chuck about Edgar Allan Poe. I wasn't sure if it would make it worse or better. What I did know was that I had won a battle, so I went to work on securing hotel reservations and tour tickets.

chapter seven

I could barely sleep that night. It was an excitement much like a four-year-old on Christmas Eve. I dreamed of roads, houses, and history that all had to do with Charleston. During the drive there, I felt as if we were going home. And as we took in the marshlands and plantations along our route, Chuck's energy became lighter and happier.

"This all looks familiar to me," he kept saying over and over.

"Me too," I said with a smile. I knew that Poe was sitting in the backseat of the car looking all smug, so I didn't dare turn around and give him any satisfaction.

Once we crossed over the New Cooper River Bridge that led us to Charleston, I was filled with emotions ranging from excitement to anticipation. We immediately found our hotel, tucked away on a quiet street only a block from the waterfront and an easy stroll to the City Market and the Battery. I had chosen the Anchorage Inn, which was located in Charleston's historic French Quarter district. Originally built as a cotton warehouse in 1840, it was turned into a B & B in 1991, and it had no references to hauntings on any websites. I was trying to keep my end of the bargain. Although I was a ghost magnet and had an entourage of spirit guides with me, I could only keep the promise going so far.

After checking into our hotel, we raced into the town to catch our horse and carriage history tour. As soon as we parked and I looked around at the marketplace, I began to sniffle. I looked over at Chuck to see if he had the same emotion and was instead met with an odd stiffness, like preparing to go in front of family that you haven't seen since an argument. It was only 10:00 o'clock in the morning, but the temperatures were already beginning to heat up, and being that both Chuck and I were animal lovers we thought about canceling as we couldn't get over the fact that the poor horses would have to carry us through the streets in the heat. But we ended up going anyhow after the tour company promised us that they would stop several times to give them water and some rest in the shade.

As we began down the brick streets, our guide gave us a bit of Charleston history. And both Chuck and I began to tear up. It was hard to explain, but we knew we were home. Not of this lifetime, but another.

In 1670, a group of British settlers arrived at the tip end of the Charleston peninsula, which today is referred to as Battery Park. Within just a few years, the settlers began to construct the charming city that was originally called Charles Town to honor England's Charles II. It became one of America's leading cities.

At that same time, pirates began to take advantage of the waterways. One of the most infamous, Blackbeard, earned a reputation as a ruthless pirate. He terrorized sailors and ambushed passenger and cargo ships. Many times the crew would simply surrender without a fight. The time was duly referred to as the reign of terror. The climax of Blackbeard's reign of terror was in May 1718, when Blackbeard held a weeklong blockade at the port in Charleston, South Carolina. Blackbeard commanded over 400 pirates and several ships of which he lined up across the bay in Charleston. For several weeks he held the city hostage, demanding food, money, and supplies. Legend had it that Blackbeard had a dramatic flair and would dress as a woman, high heels and all, and go into town.

Following the reign of terror on Charleston, Blackbeard surprisingly surrendered and promised to stop his criminal ways. He married his fourteenth wife and took up residency in the Outer Banks of North Carolina, but it wasn't long before he was back at his pirate ways, frightening sailors enough that they wouldn't take to sea. He was finally captured and killed at sea in the Outer Banks.

Besides the pirates, the military and the shipping industry took advantage of Charleston's prime location of rivers and its proximity to the Atlantic Ocean. They utilized it for slave trade and rice shipments. In 1861, the first shots of the Civil War were fired off the peninsula at Fort Sumter.

Today, Charleston is known for paper and cigar manufacturing. Its rich history and architecture make it a tourism gem. With an eclectic culture, Charleston is also known for being one of the friendliest cities in America.

As the carriage rounded the corner, it came to a complete stop at Battery Park, also known as White Point. On one side of the street stood stunning mansions overlooking the park with cascading palmettos and large oak trees, cannons from the Civil War, and the waterway. The guide further pointed out that White Point was where dozens of pirates were hanged from oak trees and gallows in the early 1700s and left dangling from their nooses for days to try to scare off other potential pirates. But it wasn't the potential pirate hauntings that caught my attention, but one particular mansion. She stood in all of her glory, hidden ever slightly by amazing landscaping and gardens. Honeysuckle vines dressed the wrought iron fence that protected her from tourists. Before I could say anything, the carriage was on to its next destination. I was caught up in my thoughts when the guide's next words caught my attention.

"And right over there is Fort Sumter, well-known to any Edgar Allan Poe fans. This was where he was stationed."

How didn't I realize that? I thought. Poe *did* have a Charleston connection. And here I was just indulging in my own past life not realizing that there might be dots to be connected. I would have to come clean with Chuck. Although not a psychic, he had great intuition and good detective skills. And he believed in me.

The history tour continued for over an hour and let us out right where we began. I went over and gave our horses a final pat goodbye when the company announced they were going to close for the rest of the day because of the high temperatures. All I could think was that I almost chose a later time, and something told me to book it early. Was it pure luck or universal synchronicity?

"What now?" Chuck asked, looking around, as if soaking everything into his memory.

"Let's do lunch and go shopping, then maybe a nap so that we aren't dead for tonight's ghost tour. No pun."

Chuck grinned and grabbed my hand as we walked around the center of town. We finally agreed on a small diner that offered sandwiches with thick, homemade bread, cold cuts, and freshly grown tomatoes.

A large black lady with rosy cheeks smiled wide at me across the counter. "Welcome home, Kristy!" She was an older woman with her hair held tight with a hair net and she came around the counter and offered me a welcoming hug. Her drawl was mixed with a Jamaican and Southern accent. She simply smiled at me, said she was happy to see me, and went back across the counter.

"Excuse me?" I asked, looking at Chuck to see if he was paying any attention, but he was busy studying the menu.

"What can I get you?" She continued smiling warmly at me.

I slowly shook my head, sure that I must've imagined it. I ordered a ham with cheddar cheese on white bread with tomatoes and Chuck ordered corned beef with coleslaw.

"Did you hear her?" I whispered, looking over my large lemonade.

"Yep, she knew your name," my husband nonchalantly said, as if it were no big deal. "Kristy, stop trying to figure it all out."

"Did you say my name when we came in?"

Chuck gave me a warning look and just shook his head. "Nothing surprises me with you anymore, I don't know why it does you," he laughed.

Maybe he was right, but to feel as if I was plopped in the middle of a *Twilight Zone* episode was freaking me out just a tad.

When she delivered the food to our small two-person table, she still wore her huge smile. "I'm Rose, if you need anything else." And as I ate, I watched her with the other customers. Although she was friendly, her smile wasn't as large nor did she call them by name, and she certainly didn't come around from the counter to give any of them a hug.

It was the best sandwich since my mom made me a similar one years ago before her passing. Something I missed badly about my mom—her cooking. As we were throwing our crumbs and napkins away in the wastebasket,

Rose called out a southern goodbye to us, but added my name again. Only my name. I looked her in the eyes and smiled my farewell.

The moment we stepped out into the street the sweat started to pour down our foreheads, so we decided to stroll through City Market, four blocks of an open market with vendors selling sweet grass baskets, jewelry, and everything in between. We found some prints of Charleston that we purchased along with some postcards to send to the kids. I chatted with several of the vendors who were curious as to where my accent was from.

At one point, I felt as if I was being watched and looked up to see a seated heavy lady dressed in a floral-patterned sundress and large brimmed hat staring at me. Sweet grass baskets and palmetto flowers were her expertise. I smiled and nodded at her, but she continued to stare at me with what seemed to be a knowing. Finally, after what felt like ages, she broke into a smile that felt reminiscent of a pained friend who felt abandoned but couldn't hold on to the anger for fear of losing the love. I smiled back, tears forming in both of our eyes. I stopped to compliment her on her gift. She simply continued smiling as if to say that I had finally returned home. After an hour of perusing trinkets and knickknacks, we grabbed a Coke and decided to make our way back to the water and find some shade to sit. Every so often I checked to see if Poe was with me, but I didn't see him, nor did I see Alto, and I wondered what trouble they might be causing.

As we walked, without any map in hand or knowledge or direction as to where we were going, we came upon a graveyard. Large trees acted as a canopy from the heat and the bright sunshine, so we snuck away to take some photos. When we heard a roll of thunder in the distance, we glanced at one another and laughed at the spooky irony. But before we could even decide on what to do, lightning lit up the sky and the thunder grew more intense. Rain didn't fall, but the loud rumbling in the heavens made for quite the atmosphere as I perused gravestones of those I believed to be my ancestors from a life undocumented. Was it perhaps a sign or was I overdramatizing it? We continued on our journey through the graveyard that almost appeared to be abandoned with its tall grass and out-of-control shrubs. After exploring, we decided to head toward the park.

Just as we found the park, the storm intensified and we found ourselves sitting on an aluminum bench in a haunted park under a bunch of trees. Not the smartest place to be in a storm, but it lasted mere moments. We watched as the dark clouds blew out to sea and we were left once more with bright sunshine and an awful humidity.

"I think our house is around here," I said simply and with confidence.

"I think so, too. Shall we look?"

I nodded. I couldn't tell if Chuck was just trying to appease me or if he was truly feeling the past life connection, and I didn't much care to debate it. We began to walk hand in hand, carefully examining each mansion and checking in with my intuition. I knew that the house I was looking for didn't have a clear view of the water, but that the park was in front of it, so it helped to limit our search. I felt pulled to an antebellum mansion on Broad Street and instead of feeling satisfied, I began to cry with a soul ache that spanned lifetimes. Chuck just held me.

"I'd like to find out the history of this house," I said. And just as I finished the sentence a woman, who had on a shirt representing a local tour, passed by and offered us a suggestion of how to go about doing that.

I didn't want to appear too crazy, but I started rambling about a past life, and she nodded and smiled. "I get it. That is why I moved here from New York. I get it." She wished us luck and continued on.

I jotted down the address and snapped a photo. Then we decided to head back to the hotel and take a nap, catch dinner, and then await the ghost tour.

Walking along the waterfront toward our inn, I felt a pull across the waterway where the tour guide had pointed out Fort Sumter.

"Reynolds," the wind whispered.

I whipped around to see if someone was around me, namely Poe, but saw nobody in human or spirit form except for Chuck, who was sitting on a park bench taking photos of a squirrel that was eating someone's throwaway lunch.

I shrugged, thinking I was possibly energy raw from the past few days. I joined my husband and we began walking again, hand in hand, enjoying the salt air and warm breeze when I once again heard the name called out. This time it came out teasing and sing-songy, but again, nobody was there. I shook my head, wondering if I just needed to see a doctor when I returned home—either a psychologist or a neurologist or both.

Between the tears and the varied emotions, I dozed quickly into a soundless nap and woke up to my alarm. After a hot shower and a change of clothes, we made our way to the entrance of the ghost tour. Now, even though I give ghost tours myself and I am a medium, I like to go more for the history of the haunt, and not necessarily to see anything. In fact, it was rare that I ever saw anything on these types of tours.

We met up with the tour guide, who was all decked out in costume and carrying a gas lantern, along with a handful of people, including one woman who was just plain pissed off that her kids talked her into going.

"There's no such thing as ghosts," she exclaimed two dozen or more times until another on the tour finally told her to either join us or shut up. And surprisingly it wasn't Chuck! She quieted, but her energy was dark and her eyes continued to roll around in her head as our tour guide dramatically told the stories.

The guide first took us into two alleyways. The first narrow, cobblestone alleyway was where Colonial and Revolutionary men would fight with pistols and swords to their death. The last was named Lodge Alley after the Freemasons and was paved with Belgian blocks. It allowed access for sailors to and from their homes and the wharf.

As I listened to the guide's tales, I could feel a presence in Lodge Alley and felt the need to snap a photo when the lady who continued to spout that ghosts were figments of anyone's imagination yelped.

"Someone pushed me!"

But she stood there alone, arms crossed and with a scowl on her face. When I looked at my photos, it told another story. Right next to the woman was a dark shadow with what looked like a trench coat and top hat on, possibly trying to prove to her once and for all that there was something more out there than what meets the eye. She and her kids promptly left the tour. I also recognized the dark shadow to be none other than my mischievous spirit guide, Edgar Allan Poe.

I was snickering (I know, probably not nice) when the tour guide asked to see my photo, and then Chuck decided to announce to her that I was a medium. She had probably heard that a time or two and didn't seem impressed, but we chatted about psychic experiences as we made it to our final stop—the gates of the Unitarian Cemetery.

The Unitarian Cemetery is notably haunted, and although the legends and lore vary with each storyteller, the person haunting the cemetery remains the same—Annabel Lee.

The legend begins before the Civil War when a Virginia sailor stationed in Charleston, South Carolina, met a local Charleston girl named Annabel Lee Revanel. They quickly fell in love, which dismayed Annabel's father, who forbade Annabel to see the sailor because he was from the North. So, Annabel would sneak out to meet the sailor in the secluded Unitarian Cemetery. Their secret meetings continued until one day Annabel's father grew suspicious and followed his daughter. Enraged at the unavowed romance, he locked Annabel in her room for several months, making any further meeting impossible. The sailor was devastated.

It was just a few months later when the sailor received a letter from a comrade who knew of his romance, letting him know that Annabel died from yellow fever. He made plans at once to attend the funeral, to give his love a final goodbye. Annabel's father, however, blamed the sailor for the death of his daughter, for if it weren't for that sailor he would've never had to lock her away and therefore she would've not gotten sick. In a gesture of revenge, knowing that the sailor would return and attempt to visit the cemetery and gravesite of his daughter, he ordered that there be six graves dug up in the family plot so when the sailor arrived he wouldn't know exactly where his true love lay.

The sailor returned to the cemetery on the day of the funeral to find that his love's father hired guards. So he went to the local tavern awaiting his time to give his final farewell. Once the memorial was over and everyone departed, he went into the cemetery to find the act of vengeance and he left with despair and sadness.

The sailor? Edgar Allan Poe. The poem he would later write was "Annabel Lee."

As the guide finished her tale, a silent cat caught our attention. Lying on top of the roof, he simply listened to the story, his paws stretched out and looking bored. We all laughed at the odd sight. The guide wished us well and pointed toward our lodging. I was still stuck on the story, wondering why Poe wouldn't have told me about the legend and if perhaps this had something to do with why he urged us to come.

What now? I wondered. What did it all mean, and what was I supposed to do with the information? I looked to see the tour guide standing there looking out over the cemetery, next to her was Poe, sentimentally gazing, and the cat had climbed down from the rooftop and was standing in the alleyway inside the cemetery.

I sat down on the step and shivered as the night wrapped around me.

"You cold?" Chuck asked, putting his arm around me in a protective way.

"No, not cold," I mumbled, confused.

Chuck raised an eyebrow in question. Chuck knew that our adventure dealt with past lives, our past lives, but he was unaware of the Edgar Allan Poe connection. He knew how much I loved Poe's work, and he knew who most of my guides were, but he didn't know that Poe was included in my crazy group. And honestly, how does one start that conversation?

"Do you think…? No, it's silly to think…" The tour guide caught me off guard.

The cat slinked from the back alley of the cemetery and sat just a few feet from us, as if joining in on the conversation.

The tour guide walked slowly to us, the cat unmoving. "You know, I tell this story every night, and every single night during the same story a cat joins in. I've been doing this tour for years. It isn't always the same cat, but a cat nonetheless. I have always wondered if it was perhaps…you'll think this is crazy," she laughed.

"Honestly, I won't think it's crazy."

"Do you think this is Poe? I don't know why I never think it is Annabel, but I don't. Do you think it is Poe?" she asked again.

I nodded. I did. I didn't believe that he was the reincarnated cat, but I believed his spirit visited within the cat. Poe sat on the park bench outside the cemetery gates now and the cat noticed him, walked over, and rubbed against his legs. Poe bent down and petted the cat, looked over at me, and nodded in agreement. He said, "I wish I could write as mysterious as a cat." Then, he grinned mischievously at me. Poe loved animals and even had his own cat with his wife Virginia that he doted on, believed to be a tortoiseshell, named Catterina.

"Yeah, it makes a whole lot of sense."

The cat, finally bored with the conversation, walked over to the gateway to the moonlit cemetery. It turned as if to say goodbye then disappeared into the night.

A fog slowly began to cascade along Archdale Street and we took that as a sign to walk back. The streets were completely empty as the three of us, deep in thought, made our way back to town. I gave in to temptation and looked back only to see the cat sitting in the center of the brick-laid street, watching, and Poe gone.

"Funny since that was the cemetery the storm began in earlier, huh?" Chuck pondered.

I could only nod.

Chuck and I said our final goodbye to our guide and made our way back to the hotel, walking in silence until we walked back into our room.

"Got something to tell me about Edgar Allan Poe, Kristy?"

"He's a fine literary figure from our past?" I smiled, trying to look innocent.

"And anything else?"

"There's more, that is for sure, but I need to try and put it together. I promise I will share, just not right now."

Chuck was quite intuitive, although he would never claim to have a psychic ability. It was the intuitive bond that we both had that made our relationship strong, and sometimes even annoying.

"I don't have a mind of my own!" Chuck would cry after I finished his thoughts out loud.

I would just shrug and laugh. But the Edgar Allan Poe part of my life, although I felt bad that I was keeping it under wraps, had to stay secret. I was still trying to connect more dots.

We both climbed in our pajamas and snuggled up in the ivory lace canopy bed that looked out over the cobble-stone streets of Charleston and fell fast asleep.

Chuck and I stayed only one night in Charleston. That twenty-four hours helped put to rest some questions that were deep within my soul, but they replaced them with even more. The only disappointment was the length of time it took for me to listen to the song within my soul. Poe had led me to Chuck. He had led me to Baltimore, Asheville, and now Charleston. And although I felt at home here, I felt unsettled to know that I would have to leave without all of the answers.

On the ride home I continued to remind Chuck that I had kept my promise. We didn't have any haunted experiences at the hotel. He just rolled his eyes in response to me.

Annabel Lee
Edgar Allan Poe

It was many and many a year ago,
    In a kingdom by the sea,
That a maiden there lived whom you may know
    By the name of Annabel Lee;—
And this maiden she lived with no other thought
    Than to love and be loved by me.

I was a child and *she* was a child,
    In this kingdom by the sea;
But we loved with a love that was more than love—
    I and my Annabel Lee—
With a love that the wingéd seraphs in Heaven
    Coveted her and me.

And this was the reason that, long ago,
    In this kingdom by the sea,

A wind blew out of a cloud chilling
    My beautiful Annabel Lee;
So that her high-born kinsman came
    And bore her away from me,
To shut her up, in a sepulchre,
    In this kingdom by the sea.

The angels, not half so happy in Heaven,
    Went envying her and me—
Yes!—that was the reason (as all men know,
    In this kingdom by the sea)
That the wind came out of the cloud by night,
    Chilling and killing my Annabel Lee.

But our love it was stronger by far than the love
    Of those who were older than we—
    Of many far wiser than we—
And neither the angels in Heaven above,
    Nor the demons down under the sea,
Can ever dissever my soul from the soul
    Of the beautiful Annabel Lee:—

For the moon never beams, without bringing me dream
    Of the beautiful Annabel Lee;
And the stars never rise, but I feel the bright eyes
    Of the beautiful Annabel Lee:—
And so, all the night-tide, I lie down by the side
Of my darling—my darling—my life and my bride,
    In her sepulchre there by the sea—
    In her tomb by the sounding sea.

chapter eight

I sat in the hotel room in nowhere West Virginia as Chuck scavenged for food. We had driven over seven hours toward home, but we were physically exhausted, more so emotionally spent, and we knew we couldn't drive straight through to Michigan. However, searching for a vacant room took well over an hour since every hotel was booked—mainly because there just weren't any hotels in the area as it was pretty desolate. I wondered if our dinner might not be cookies and chips from the vending machine down the hall.

After changing into my cotton pajamas, I turned on the small RCA television and crawled under the itchy and loud flowered bedspread that covered the full-size bed. I was startled when I heard a throat clear. Propping myself up with two uncomfortable foam pillows, I looked over to see Poe sitting in the gray tweed desk chair staring out the window at the sunset that had colored the sky pink.

"I'm tired, Edgar," I said flatly, grabbing my glasses off the nightstand and putting them on. I was almost legally blind without my contacts or glasses.

"And testy, too," Poe added, grinning back at me while smoothing his dark hair back with his left hand.

"You must be wearing off on me." I took a deep breath and bit my tongue so not to say anything more.

Poe laughed heartily. There was something about him that felt lighter, and I wondered if perhaps I had extracted his normal moodiness with my empathic ability. I moaned out loud at the thought, which only made Poe cackle louder.

"I promise that I won't bother you for long, I just wanted to be a tattle."

I raised my left eyebrow at him in question.

"Alto's missing," Poe crowed.

"What? Are guides allowed to split?" I bit my bottom lip, trying not to panic. Alto has been my guide since birth and he was my most helpful and sensible guide. This wasn't like him. "What did you do to him, Edgar? Did you piss him off?"

"I am insulted that you would think such a thing!" Poe huffed. "He said something about reconnecting with his ancestors."

From the stories Alto had told me, when he was alive he originally lived in the Carolinas. It all made sense. Ever since we had passed the North Carolina border on the way to Asheville, I had stopped feeling his presence. And then there were the oddities with the séance at the Reynolds

Mansion. Alto, who always acted as my spirit guard, didn't. He was also in charge of making sure that my business continued and that I had clients, yet I hadn't received one booked client since I left Michigan. He planned this all along. I was ticked off.

"Looks like I am your mainstay."

I groaned, threw the pillow over my head, and pretended to suffocate myself when I heard Chuck unlock the door. Although I was starving, the smell of the pizza mixed with Poe's announcement made me feel instantly nauseous, and I think I turned a shade of green.

"Are you okay?" Chuck looked at me, puzzled.

I swung my legs off the side of the bed and pushed the blankets away. Chuck gave me a peck on my cheek and handed me a piece of ham pizza that, although feeling physically ill, I graciously took a big bite of. "I will be. I just need nourishment and sleep." *And for Alto to come back*, I said silently in my head.

"No, seriously, you look like you've seen a ghost."

Normally Chuck didn't press, so I thought it best to just tell him. He knew about Alto and Tallie, just not Edgar. I knew that it still wasn't the right time to confess, so I said what I knew he would understand.

"Alto's gone."

"Like he's been kidnapped? Or we lost him en route? He couldn't have died; he's already dead." He scratched his cheek in confusion, smearing tomato sauce on it, which made me laugh and broke some tension. I took a napkin and wiped it away.

"Are guides allowed to do that?" he asked.

"I think he took a vacation without telling me."

"After forty years with you, I'm sure he needed it," I heard Poe sarcastically interject telepathically to me.

I agreed with him. What a frustrating job my guides had. Maybe I shouldn't be so angry. But really, couldn't he have at least forewarned me? Alto was the strong and quiet type, but he was also dedicated to a fault. But to leave me with Poe, who probably flirted erroneously with Tallie so that she decided to jet, too. I wasn't seeing or feeling her much lately either.

"What are you going to do?" Chuck asked, taking another bite of his pizza. I looked over to where Poe had been sitting to see if he might have a suggestion, but I found only an empty seat.

"I'm not sure," I sighed, throwing my half-eaten pizza away in the garbage. I plopped back down on the bed, hoping the ceiling would miraculously have an answer written on it. It didn't. I would just have to deal with the missing-in-action guide when I got home. Or hope that he would show up from his holiday soon.

It would be another two weeks before Alto came back, but not before I put a call out that if he didn't show up as soon as possible he would be replaced. And secretly while Alto was gone I held out hope that he would return quickly because Poe was driving me nuts and I needed my reliable, go-to guide to help me deal with him.

Just as Alto decided to show up for Spirit Guide duty, Poe came to me demanding another trip.

"We have to do what?" I asked, agitated.

"You have to go back to Baltimore," Poe repeated.

I held my head, feeling a headache coming on. "Sure, I can just hop on a plane and tell the family that I have business in Baltimore when I don't. How exactly do you want me to explain this?"

Poe had already thought up an intricate plan and was ready to pounce on me the moment I questioned him.

Just a few months beforehand, Chuck and I had traveled to Gettysburg. "Haunted locations are where most everyone spends their anniversary, right? Or maybe that's just us," I had commented over and over during our trip. I had also said that the kids needed to visit, so Poe thought that a combined trip—flying into Baltimore, driving to Gettysburg, and then driving back to Baltimore would fit quite well with his scheme. And seeing how much I loved and adored Gettysburg, he had me there. But just to make him sweat, I contested.

"Nope. I have no money nor do I have time, Edgar. It won't," I looked him straight in the eyes, "and cannot work." Walking away from him without offering him a chance to debate it gave me the upper hand. Or at least that was how I saw it.

For several months Poe continued to beg for me to make the trip, and I continued to defend my original decision. But secretly I was plotting in my head how to instigate the trip with Chuck. I, too, felt the need to get back to Fell's Point, walk the cobblestone streets, and visit the alleyway. I wanted to challenge my visions and empathic mediumship. There were answers to some of the secrets that I felt needed to be shared, so I decided to use that as leverage.

It was still dusk when I climbed out of bed. Chuck's CPAP machine breathed in and out, helping Chuck to not snore and to sleep deeply. He didn't move when my white and gray Siamese kitten climbed into my place and snuggled up next to him.

Without turning on any lights, I sat on the red couch in my living room, my mind filled with worry and wonder. I could feel my guides around me and thought this might be the best time to have a heart-to-heart with Poe.

"Tell me about Reynolds, Edgar, and I will think about talking to Chuck about a trip," I asserted.

The morning was a gloomy one and instead of sunshine, storm clouds rolled in. Poe stood in front of me with a blank look on his face at first. Then, he mumbled something about me being incorrigible but nonetheless sat down on the living room's paisley-patterned armchair and began.

"First we have to discuss Mary Rogers."

"The premise of your book *The Murders of Rue Morgue*?"

Poe puffed his chest out and smiled.

"This case, and your book, is still mentioned in criminology classes, Edgar. When I took Introduction to Criminal Justice at the university, your book and this case was one of the first discussions, along with the introduction of the notion of *ratiocination*—the exercise of reason in the process of analyzing clues."

"And so it should be," he proudly added to my eye roll. "Can I begin now, or would you like to share the story with *me*?"

I smirked and made a motion that I was zipping my lips.

"Mary Cecilia Rogers was a stunningly beautiful brunette and a charming twenty-year-old. She was hired to stand behind the cigar counter but for one reason: to attract men, which ultimately worked. She was easy to talk to, and even more so, easy to look at. However, she wasn't the brightest girl."

I laughed. "It sounds like maybe Mary is Kim Kardashian reincarnated."

Poe looked at me with a puzzled look and sighed. He had been with me long enough now to realize I didn't sit quietly through stories.

"But it was the summer of 1841 when she became the talk of the town. Not for her beauty, but for her death.

"Born in 1820, Mary lived a comfortable life in Connecticut until her father and three of her half brothers died and her mother had to sell their property and relocate to New York City. There, Mary and her extraordinary looks came to the attention of John Anderson. He was a young entrepreneur who was looking for a gimmick for his newest business, Anderson's Tobacco Emporium. He hired Mary at a generous wage to work, smile, and flirt behind the cigar counter. The store catered to professionals, mostly that of writers, reporters, and those working in the city's nearby government offices. Mary's so-called fame made her notorious and thrust her into the limelight, which made her uncomfortable, or maybe more so made her mother uncomfortable, if not maybe even jealous. What truly happened was John Anderson and Mary were having an affair and her family was dissatisfied with the arrangement. The very reason he hired Mary was making him horribly jealous. When one of her half brothers claimed some riches and opened a boarding house, she moved on to help him with his business, but within a year he, too, would die.

"No matter where Mary went, her fame followed, though. Soon Mary had two very serious suitors—Alfred Crommelin, a tall, handsome, and polite man who had been a boarder at the house, and Daniel Payne, a common worker who was a cork cutter by trade. Her mother also detested Daniel, who had no money and was an alcoholic, but Mary didn't care about that. She fell in love with Daniel and accepted his hand in marriage after previously being engaged to Alfred."

"Now that sounds scandalous in itself," I added.

Poe ignored me and continued.

"On July 25, 1841, a Sunday morning, Mary went to Daniel's apartment and told him she was going to visit her aunt. She asked Daniel to meet with her early that evening. That evening a severe storm rolled in, and when Mary didn't show up Daniel thought perhaps Mary stayed overnight to wait out the storm. But Mary never showed up the next day. When Daniel went to her aunt's house, she was unaware that Mary was to make a visit at all.

"It is here that it gets a bit complicated," Poe warned.

I was sitting on the edge of my seat. I always loved a good mystery, and one of the best storytellers was sharing the tale with me.

"Mary's so-called mother, her current fiancé Daniel, and her former fiancé Alfred Crommelin all searched without results."

"Wait," I held up my hand to stop him, "what do you mean *so-called* mother?"

"Oh, apparently promiscuity ran in that family. Mary's mother was actually her grandmother. Mary's true mother was more than likely her mother's eldest daughter from her first marriage."

"Did she know that?" I asked, thinking how skeletons were buried deep in every family, in every time period.

Poe nodded. "She had to. Phoebe would've been forty years old when she had Mary. Now can I continue?"

I made a gesture for him to get on with it.

"In a panic, an ad was placed in the newspaper asking for any information on the whereabouts of Mary Rogers and to please inform her mother. Because of Mary's past profession as the Cigar Girl, and her interaction with the many newspaper reporters and editors, the story quickly became a media frenzy and made headlines.

"She had previously disappeared before."

"What?" I asked, stunned.

"Yes, just a few days before this incident. Her mother claimed that she found an apparent suicide note and took it to the police only to discover that Mary was visiting with friends."

"Was it a suicide note?" I asked, confused.

"No," he dryly replied.

"And did you know Mary personally?"

Poe nodded. "I was living in Hoboken at the time. Would you please just let me continue?"

I sighed and gave him a thumbs-up.

"It was that Wednesday after Mary went missing when she was found by two men from Hoboken, New Jersey. In an attempt to cool down from the hot summer day, they had taken refuge by Sybil's Cave, a popular spot on the Hudson River. They spotted something floating in the shallow waters, ran down the dock, and borrowed a boat to see what it might be. Their attempt to fish it out helped to make the discovery of Mary Rogers's badly beaten and decomposed body.

"The coroner's report was grisly. Mary's angelic face had been badly beaten. There were finger indentations around her neck, along with a garotte of lace from Mary's clothing that was submerged in her skin and tied in a sailor's knot. Her hands had been tied and her back was raw, which indicated that she had been dragged for quite a distance. Fabric from her clothing was used to strangulate her and used as a gag. Finally, there were bruises and abrasions covering her private areas."

"She had been raped?" I asked in disgust.

Poe once again glowered at me.

"Sorry," I mumbled.

"The coroner described the corpse in his report as '… *her face was swollen, the veins were highly distended. There was a mark about the size and shape of a man's thumb on the right side of the neck, near the jugular vein, and two or three marks on the left side resembling the shape of a man's fingers, which led me to believe she had been throttled and partially choked by a man's hand. It appeared as if the wrists had been tied together, and as if she had raised her hands to try to tear something from off her mouth and neck, which was choking and strangling her. The dress was much torn in several places…a piece was torn clean out of this garment, about a foot or 18 inches in width…this same piece was tied round her mouth, with a hard knot at the back part of the neck; I think this was done to smother her cries and that it was probably held tight round her mouth by one of her brutal ravishers. Her hat was off her head at the time of the outrage, and that after her violation and murder had been completed, it was tied on.'*

"Furthermore, the doctor concluded that in no way had she been pregnant and believed that more than two or three people had committed the horrible murder.

"Newspaper editors and those associated with the *Penny Press*, which was much like a tabloid magazine today," Poe explained, "many of which knew Mary, had a field day with the reports. They began reporting their own theories, as New York at that time was becoming unruly and even dangerous with a large amount of immigrants and gangs. But to make matters worse, there wasn't a police force, so instead a group of constables and magistrates gathered together to bumble their way in hopes of solving the case and publicly charged every one of Mary's suitors, and there were many, but they were all cleared.

"Mrs. Frederica Loss ran a tavern called Nick Moore's House in the woodlands near Hoboken, not far from where Mary Roger's body had been brought to shore. Her smart business sense with the tavern earned her enough money to buy several acres where she raised her three less-than-stellar sons.

"One month after Mary's disappearance, on August 25, 1841, two of her boys were supposedly collecting sassafras bark when they discovered articles of women's clothing, including a handkerchief monogrammed M. R. and women's gloves. They immediately brought the mildewed and crumpled items to their mother. It would be a week or so before Mrs. Loss contacted the authorities."

"Why?" I asked, confused.

"Think about it, Kristy. Use logic. With Frederica Loss's new celebrity status, her tavern became the hot spot for spectators. She made a statement to police that she had seen Mary on the day of her disappearance with a man of 'dark complexion.' She said that they came into her inn at about 4:00 on the afternoon of Sunday, July 25, and the landlady served them refreshments: liquor for the man and lemonade for Mary. Loss went on to say that she heard a scream in the evening and thought it was one of her sons. She later forgot about it all when she found her children safe."

"That sounds fishy for sure!"

"It was. Loss's story began to disintegrate, especially when the *Herald* reported that Mary Rogers was wearing gloves when her body was discovered and it was unclear why there would be another pair of gloves found in the thicket on Loss's property."

"It was Mary's ghost that began to unravel many. And maybe still does," Poe added.

"Even you?" I squinted and looked at him.

He swallowed hard and continued.

"Mary's fiancé, Daniel Payne, plunged into a deep grief after Mary's death. The already alcoholic cork cutter drank even more heavily and his brother feared that Daniel was slowly going insane."

I was going to say something witty but thought it best not to interrupt again.

"In the weeks following Mary's death, Payne was under suspicion in her death because of the *Tattler*'s assertion that the body taken from the Hudson was not Mary Rogers at all and Payne had to identify her body. It was soon after that when Payne confessed to many that Mary's ghost was visiting him. Most people assumed that it was the spirits—as in alcohol—and not really Mary's spirit. It all became too much for him and on the morning of October 7, 1841, Payne left his New York lodging, caught a ferry to Hoboken, and stopped in Loss's tavern. He asked for directions to the thicket where his love's clothing had been found, and on his way purchased a small bottle of the poison laudanum and some brandy. Sitting next to the thicket, he took out a piece of paper and wrote: *To the World—here I am on the very spot. May God forgive me for my misspent life.* Putting the note into his pocket, he quickly consumed the poison."

"And he died there?"

"Not yet..."

"Laudanum took some time to work, apparently, so Payne went back to Loss's tavern for more liquor. He finally stumbled back to the place where Mary's body had been brought ashore. He lay down on a bench there and died."

I held up my hand to once again stop Poe. This all was just too similar to Poe's own passing. It was all becoming a bit clear to me. "He was poisoned. He didn't commit suicide," I cried.

Poe ignored my outburst. "His suicide brought the Mary Rogers case back to the headlines, although his cryptic note was seen as an admission of guilt as his murderer had hoped. Plus, he had an iron-tight alibi and numerous witnesses who saw him on that fateful day. But murder was not at all what anybody thought. Instead, they saw him as a love-struck romantic who could not bear life without his Mary."

"What happened to Frederica?"

"In October 1842, innkeeper Frederica Loss was accidently shot by one of her sons."

"There are an awful lot of accidents," I sarcastically said.

"For over two weeks Frederica lay on her deathbed, in and out of consciousness, and often shouting at the ghost of Mary Rogers. In her last moments, Ross confessed that Mary Rogers and a young 'dark and tall' doctor arrived at her inn on that Sunday and Mary had an abortion performed, from which Mary died of complications. Frederica said that her son assisted in sinking Mary's body in the river where it was found. Mary's clothing was discarded in a neighbor's pond, but afterward thought unsafe, so it was found and scattered through the woods."

"And that is what you ran with in your second mystery. Detective Chevalier C. Auguste Dupin believed the murderer and the lover to have been a naval officer of dark complexion who had previously attempted to elope with Mary, or Marie," I corrected, "Dupin believed that he killed her the next time they saw one another. Did you honestly believe that to be the truth?"

"Who are you talking to?"

I jumped and grabbed my chest. Chuck stood in the doorway between the living room and kitchen just staring at me, curiously.

I blushed. "I am going over a new story I am thinking of writing," I explained, pointing to the notebook in my lap.

Chuck scratched his gray whiskers on his chin and grinned cockeyed. Walking over to me, he kissed me on the nose. "You would tell me if you were planning on killing me, right?" he joked.

"Oh, for sure," I laughed.

"It's a good thing I'm okay with weird, Kristy." He walked into the hallway and into the bathroom.

"You have no idea," I mumbled. Noticing that Poe had disappeared, I decided to make some blueberry muffins for breakfast. Baking had a way of soothing my nerves.

I was a ball of nerves that whole day waiting to hear the rest of Poe's story. With my busy life, that wouldn't happen till later that evening. Then the kids were busy in their rooms, Chuck had crashed on the couch in front of a Detroit Tigers baseball game, and that gave me time to escape.

"You know that there was, and still is, speculation that you were Mary's murderer," I began our conversation. It made me wonder for a split second if guides were allowed to be criminals. Could it possibly be a way to help with karma? I shook the thought out of my head.

Poe huffed. "I loved and lost. I never loved and murdered—except in my stories," he added with a wink and a sideways grin.

"So…tell me the *real* story," I prodded, grabbing an ivory cable-knit blanket off the back of the couch, wrapping it around me and preparing myself for story time.

"I did know Mary," he confessed. "Most every male that worked in that area knew her. She was hard to miss. Her bright smile and effervescent personality, well she had an innocence about her that made men want to take care of her," Poe shrugged.

I eyed him with curiosity, but before I could ask the question he held up his hand. "No, Kristy, I didn't have an affair with her. But I had taken her to dinner one night not long before she went missing. We discussed our very dysfunctional families and our even more misadjusted lives."

I thought for a moment, feeling a tad bit like Nancy Drew. Carefully I began, "Edgar, do you think that perhaps someone saw you with Mary and thought she was a threat—and killed her because of you. And killed her boyfriend just the same?"

Poe grinned with pride. "Now you are beginning to understand how to properly reason."

His grin disappeared just as quickly as it appeared.

"You feel guilty don't you, Edgar?"

"Yes, Kristy. I do. Although I did not kill her, she was murdered because of me. And that puts blood on my hands just the same."

My stomach felt sick, and I wasn't so sure I wanted to hear the remainder of the story, but I knew that whether I was prepared or not, he was going to share it with me. I rested my hand on my soured stomach and nodded for Poe to continue.

"Well, you know how sensitive I am..."

"Wait. What? Sensitive or insane?"

"Both," Poe jested. "I knew that she was having a difficult time after leaving her job at the cigar shop and how disastrous her family life was. I thought I would engage her with my company over food and drink to help cheer her. Honestly, who wouldn't want some time with me?"

My sick stomach churned, now because of Poe's overly blown ego.

"It was small talk, and I bored quickly," Poe conjured up his memory. "But she was a sweet girl, with many dreams, all of which were being contained by who she called her mother. She wished to travel and she wished to love, but not to the men whom she was betrothed. She asked for my assistance in finding her a means to travel."

"Travel to where?" I questioned.

"She didn't much care." Poe shrugged. "Somewhere, anywhere that nobody knew of her. Funny how so many want that celebrity status and yet many who have it try to run away from it."

I understood that all too much through Poe's own stories. He sorely wanted to be recognized, but at what cost? It sounded as if Mary had gone through a similar ordeal.

"I saw a man sitting in a leather cushioned seat near the doorway of the tavern. He was shrouded by shadows, with a strong chin that he raised proudly, as if already savoring a victory. He looked like an obsessed fan, the way he stared at us. But was he an admirer of mine or possibly one of Mary's? I wasn't sure which at that time. I all but ignored it and forgot about it—until she was noted as missing."

"Don't tell me that you were at Loss's Tavern."

"We were."

We all have our own quiet obsessions. Something that grabs our eye, holds our attention, or simply pulls at our heart. Something we can't help but look at. I'm not sure if it's because we are looking for something, or if the something is looking for us. But regardless, we all feel it. That pull, or that whisper that softly beckons us, and no matter how we try to steer clear of the obsession, we become even more obsessed. My obsession has always been figuring out the whodunit. I knew that was one of the major bonds Edgar Allan Poe and I shared.

"I had hoped that when she was reported missing she had just taken off for a new life. Until they found her body."

I could sense Poe's remorse, even after so many years.

"I began my research to find out who he was after offering the information to the police and finding that the police were close to nonexistent and those who pretended to be law officers were incompetent."

"Sounds like not much has changed," I smirked.

Poe's shoulders slouched as he implored the memory. "Her ghost visited me, Kristy. She asked me to make what was wrong to right. It made me wonder where the boundaries which divide Life from Death lie. Shadowy and vague at best. Who shall say where the one ends, and where the other begins? And so I thought by writing her story in the only way I knew how that something would come of it."

"Well, Edgar, most women don't want it publicized that they died as a result of an abortion!" I criticized.

He hung his head. "It was merely my way of showing that she died within, from lack of having a childhood. She was whored out by her own family! And the killer within the story was in a way me because I didn't save her. Today it still remains a mystery in history books."

"But if you know the truth, Poe ... well, maybe I can help," I offered sympathetically.

Poe had a reputation for being fueled by passion, which was often interpreted as madness. He was a man who wanted justice and honesty to prevail, but he lived in a lifetime where it didn't exist. Illnesses and death were an everyday occurrence. Pirates were the norm and people owned slaves and called it good and rich. Even Poe himself was raised to see slaves as a commodity. I often wanted to debate slavery with him, but seeing as he passed away before the Civil War, I wondered if he would understand. Although we were in a different time and place, so much was the same, so much had gone unchanged.

"Or maybe it will put you in harm's way," Poe contemplated.

"After over 160 years," I laughed, "I doubt it. What, is the ghost of the killer going to come and haunt me? Or maybe I will have a curse put upon me!" I howled.

Poe shook his head and looked at me with steel eyes. I pursed my lips together with regret. But before I could allow him to continue or apologize for acting silly, my phone rang. Despite not recognizing the out-of-state number that showed on my caller ID, I answered it anyhow.

After about a fifteen-minute conversation, I hung up the phone. Poe was still staring at me with a bored look.

"That was a paranormal group in Fort Wayne, Indiana. They want me to come speak at their upcoming conference and investigate with them at a 1900s Masonic Temple. How cool is that?"

"Kristy, remember that there are no coincidences in life."

"Only pure synchronicity," I completed his thought. "What do the Freemasons have to do with Mary's murder?" I sarcastically replied.

Poe shoved an unlit candle jar off the table in an impromptu fit of rage. Guinness, my Australian Shepherd, jumped and barked at Poe, which woke Chuck up from his nap. He came storming into the living room, reprimanding the tricolored pooch. If Guinness could only talk, I just know that he would have squealed on Poe.

Great, I said in my mind to Poe. *Now you got Guinness in trouble with your juvenile behavior. If you don't want me to go to the conference I won't, but you need to talk to me. And not with means of poetry, or code, or half stories, but with the whole shebang.*

"Go, Kristy. You'll see." I heard him respond telepathically.

Angry and frustrated with Mr. Edgar Allan Poe, I told Chuck about the opportunity. He seemed just as thrilled as my famous guide.

What am I missing? I wondered. I realized that Chuck didn't love paranormal vacations as much as I did. And I knew that Indiana lent itself to being one of the most boring states in the United States, but still.

chapter nine

My suitcase was packed and Chuck and I were off to a weekend in Indiana at a paranormal conference. A room was reserved in the hotel next to the Masonic Temple, and one of my best friends was going to join us. I was super excited, except for what put a damper on my mood.

Before we left, I opened my computer, turned on the Internet, and saw three e-mails from literary agents. I was excited until I read, and re-read each of them.

> *I have received and reviewed your query. I greatly appreciate your sending your ideas to us for consideration. Because of the number of submissions our agency receives, we often are not able to take on clients who merit publication. While I believe that your ideas might have market appeal, I am not convinced that we could represent it successfully at this time.*

Rejection, rejection, and, oh, another rejection. I laid my head on the desk next the computer keyboard and sobbed. Feelings of inadequacy stabbed like a sword through my heart and at that moment I decided that I wouldn't pursue another query and take it as a sign that I wasn't supposed to be an author. My cell phone jingled as I was about to go into another fit of sobs. Picking up my cell, and anticipating more bad news, I saw a text message from my best friend asking me how I was. I replied with bitterness and negativity over my bleak situation. Instead of giving me sympathy, she told me that it made me one step closer to my agent and that the others just weren't meant to be. What? No sympathy? No poor, poor Kristy? To make matters even worse, Poe stood over me with his typical stoic look. He wasn't disappointed that I hadn't been accepted, he was ticked off that I was acting like a girl and crying.

I sorely wanted to make everybody proud of me, and I felt like I was doing just the opposite, even with my own guide who was supposed to be gently nudging me on the right path.

"What?" I asked, ready to feast on a chocolate bar. Who cared if it was 8:00 o'clock in the morning?

"Oh, I remember these days well. The dreaded rejections," Poe snickered, which angered me even more.

"Look, you didn't do well with rejection either, and from what I know, it happened often with you. Now look! You're idolized and regarded as a genius! If they just knew," I spat.

"Kristy, everybody is rejected at one point or another. Never to suffer would never to have been blessed. Walt Disney was fired by a newspaper editor because 'he lacked imagination and had no good ideas.' Van Gogh only sold one painting, but he kept painting. Charles Schultz had every cartoon he submitted rejected by his high school yearbook staff. And remember Walt, well Disney wouldn't hire him either. Lucille Ball was told she couldn't act and needed to find a new profession. Harrison Ford was told the same. 'Balding, skinny, can dance a little,' they said of Fred Astaire at his first audition. Beethoven's music teacher declared him 'hopeless' at composing. And there are countless more who continued to find that journey within themselves and succeed. But there are many of us who give in and give up. We have stifled our life because of a critic who implied we were not good enough. And yes, even me, I was rejected numerous times and I took it to heart more than I should have."

I bit my bottom lip and took in a deep breath. "Maybe that is why you are my guide—to teach me not to take it all too seriously."

"There are always possibilities, Kristy. What I have learned, and yes, we gain perspective on the other side, is that you cannot compete with others. Instead you need to keep the doors open to the possibilities. Most of the time those possibilities aren't at all what you expect, but they end up being exactly what you need, at the exact time that you need it."

I nodded. I knew that he was right. But I was tired of being rejected so much in life. You would have thought I was used to it.

I rose from my brown leather computer chair and gave Poe a hug, a rarity. I could probably count on my one hand how many times I offered him affection and I was a crazy hugger. It was also uncommon for him to give me a pep talk, but when he did, he said all the right things.

"Is there anything that I need to be warned of before tonight?" I asked him, changing the subject.

Poe nodded. His demeanor turned serious and he scowled. "Yes. Protect yourself. I will be there, though, as will Alto. Just don't be stupid."

I had a question for him that I had pondered since he first became my guide. And with him sharing that there is gained perspective once you die and cross over, my curiosity was just too much not to inquire.

"Edgar, do you believe in God?"

"Why are bringing this up now, Kristy? Don't you have that black stuff to fix on your face."

I looked in our living room mirror and saw that my waterproof mascara was running down my face. I made a mental note to look for a different brand.

"I realize that you once said that your faith was yours alone, but many of your writings are confusing as to what you do believe in. They range from atheism to Christian to being a deist to pantheism. I always wondered, seeing as you have been to the other side, and seeing as I was raised Lutheran—well, I wondered if you had a new stance on your beliefs. You are quoted as saying 'all religion, my friend, is simply evolved out of fraud, fear, greed, imagination, and poetry.' Do you still believe that?"

Poe stepped over to the picture window and turned his back to me as he spoke. "There is no doubt that my life was filled with discontent. I felt as if most all of my life I was living in a tomb, buried alive, yet still having to live somehow. Or at least going through the motions of whatever living was supposed to entail. My soul felt broken and my heart blackened by all of the death and disease that surrounded me. In fact, I wondered for most of my life if I was the curse upon my family. A cruel karmic bounty put upon my head."

It made sense to me why many of Edgar Allan Poe's stories had a reoccurring theme of being buried alive. That's how he actually felt.

"But I always believed that there was a God, or a master energy of some sort. And when I went to the other side," Poe grinned a knowing smile, "well, let's just say that the faith I had was enough to make me your guide."

I laughed. "Or do I now have the karmic bounty on my head?"

We both grinned widely at one another. My life hadn't been all peaches and cream either, and Poe knew it.

"I ask about God because having a faith base while investigating the paranormal is very important. You have to fight with the right weapons. And you have me a bit freaked out with your hesitation with me going this weekend. Am I using the right tools?"

"I'm sorry that I frightened you. Well, maybe..." Poe retracted, "Although you are smart, you do have a silly romantic side to you, even when it comes to the paranormal. There is good and evil. Balance only comes when they both exist within the same plane. And evil will attempt to fell the good. You are good, Kristy. Stay alert."

I agreed that I would. Although his words didn't comfort me, I felt oddly comforted. Sort of like when you have an argument with a friend or a spouse and you make up, even though the argument wasn't settled. A white flag was raised, and I felt a peace within my heart.

The trip to Fort Wayne was uneventful. Chuck and I fought over the radio, as he pestered me to listen to Paul McCartney and Wings and I kept switching over to anything but.

We checked into our hotel and bumped into some friends in the lobby. There was a scheduled VIP ghost hunt that night, so we didn't have much time to do anything other than catch a quick bite to eat and head over to the Mason Temple.

The Freemasons Hall was built in 1926 and stands as a monument to the ambitions of the fraternity. The building, at the time, was one of the tallest buildings in Fort Wayne with ten stories. It was built with two electric, state-of-the-art passenger elevators, one that has been updated and the other is the original. The building has four separate lodge rooms, all identical in size but thematically decorated differently according to the uses for each room. Mason Halls were, and still are, utilized as exclusive gentlemen's clubs where men enjoy the fellowship of their fraternal brothers, much like college fraternities.

It was an ominous structure against the May night sky, and even more so when we made our entrance into the terrazzo lobby. Ornate plaster, mahogany walls, wooden ceiling beams imported from England, and a pipe organ all made it seem as if time travel had in fact occurred once the large steel doors closed behind us.

An array of participants gathered in the first-floor hall. Authors, television personalities, and ghost hunt fanatics all made up a misfit group of paranormal investigators. With cameras, recorders, walkie-talkies, and various other paranormal investigation tools in hand, we created teams. And with a plan as to which floor to go to at what time, my group of three (which consisted of myself, Chuck, and Madelyn, one of my best friends) we headed to our first destination—the basement.

Originally planned to house a bowling alley, the basement of the temple was just a typical cement-floored, musty, dusty basement. Our trio first headed to the right where there was a workshop. We could hear the furnace humming, but in the back of the room we could also hear footsteps, as if someone was waiting to jump out and give us all a good scare. Although lacking professionalism, I had been on many investigations that were pure setups with a prankster ready to give the team member a scare, all for the fun of it. I headed to the back to call out their lack of ninja skills. But as I rounded the corner, nobody was there. I shined my flashlight around the back wall to see if there was an exit, but there wasn't.

They would've had to go right by me, I thought. I turned to call out to Chuck and Maddy when a dark mass formed and even dimmed the flashlight I had hanging around my neck. I swung back around, sure once more that it was going to be an actual person, but instead I was met with a figure of a man. There weren't any obvious features that I could make out except for being ebony, as if he was a cartoon colored as dark as the darkest black would allow, with several layers. But this wasn't a cartoon and he stood in front of me with a long, black trench coat and a short dark hat. If there ever was a real shadow man, I was face-to-face with him now.

I slumped to the ground and darkness fell around me. I felt as if I was slipping away, into unconsciousness, or maybe sleep, I couldn't be sure. Everything was black.

"Kristy!" I heard Chuck calling my name, but he felt far away in a tunnel.

And then I heard Poe telling me to move. To get out of the basement. To get a grip on myself. And it was as if someone reached out their hand to mine and helped me up off the ground because before I knew it, I was standing and Chuck was walking toward me with his blue flash-light, he always had a blue flashlight, shining on me.

"Did you fall?" he asked me, pointing to my dusty jeans.

"No...," I began to explain when the walkie-talkie went off alerting us that time on our current floor was over. "Nothing's here," I said, swallowing hard. Maddy look at me cockeyed as the three of us got into the ancient elevator to meet the other teams on the main floor.

I grabbed a bottled water and put on my favorite hooded sweatshirt. It had a thermal lining and although it was eighty degrees, I felt cold. Still shaken, but trying to act normal, I continued on our haunted journey. The next couple floors were interesting, but didn't offer a repeat performance. Before heading to the fifth floor, a floor that the organizers were anxious to show me, I sat down in the social room, once used for the Masons to play pool, smoke cigars, and tell fish stories.

Why would the temple be haunted, I thought, *and who is this shadow entity?* Energy impressions can become quite pronounced with tragic events such as murders, suicides, and wrongful deaths. Spiritual energy is released within the environment and, although it doesn't necessarily equate to ghosts gone wild, it can create spikes on equipment and those who are overly sensitive can sense the differences. It is like an echo that has no time or space. And it is those echoes that paranormal investigators gravitate to because it helps define, or give a reality to, the spirit world. Each one of us has our own imprint, much like our thumbprint. *Maybe good and evil had their own echo within that imprint,* I contemplated.

"There's a portal here," Poe bellowed inside my head. "Be careful going to the fifth floor. I mean it."

A portal. There are many theories that portals are like elevators to other worlds, whether those worlds include heaven or hell or something in between, I didn't know. It is theorized that within the spirit conscious- ness an entity is able to move and shift easily between locations through portals. Those portals can move, they are not constant to one place.

"And the will therein lieth, which dieth not. Who knoweth the mysteries of the will, with its vigor? For God is but a great will pervading all things by nature of its in- tentness. Man doth not yield himself to the angels, nor unto death utterly, save only through the weakness of his feeble will. Joseph Glanvill," Poe continued.

I wanted to roll my eyes at his persistence to pound in me to be careful, but seriously, how cool was it that a gothic mastermind was quoting a seventeenth-century writer? I realized that he was enforcing his message earlier about good and evil and that it continues through lifetimes.

I gathered my equipment and found Chuck and Maddy in the lobby. We pushed the elevator arrow up and waited for the squeaky doors to open before getting in. Pushing the button for the fifth floor, we grew anxious as we felt the elevator wobble and lurch. After what felt like a year, the elevator doors opened, and ever the gen- tleman, Chuck let us gals exit first. But before he could get off, the elevator doors slammed shut and his screams of *stop*, *no*, along with several swear words brought fits of giggles from both Maddy and me. Figuring that it was just a quirk of an aging elevator, we waited for Chuck to return before entering the ritual room. A few minutes later, the elevator doors opened, and again, just as Chuck went to step out, the doors slammed on him and his cuss words continued as we heard his yelling echo below us. Now we were a bit worried. Our previous laughter instead turned to slight anxiety. Once more, the doors opened and Chuck jumped out and began running down the hallway. Now, Chuck doesn't run. Nor does he jump. And he is rarely frightened. I began running toward him, darting questions along the way.

"What are you doing? Stop running. Tell me what's wrong."

All I could hear from him was, "It's chasing me. Don't get near it!"

But I didn't see anything, only Chuck sprinting down a long corridor—to where I didn't know.

Maddy and I finally caught up to him sitting in a leather chair next to a case with Scottish armor. I handed him the opened water bottle I had drank out of earlier. Visibly shaken, his eyes darkened and were darting back and forth as he shared his ordeal.

"There was something in the elevator with me. I felt it. It was trying to enter into me. Possess me and I knew it. I can't tell you how I knew it, but I did. The only way to prevent a possession was to run from it."

I put my hand to my forehead, perplexed. "What was *it?*"

"It was more than a shadow. It was evil. Demonic, even. Maybe. All I know was it was evil." He shook his head as if trying to shake the experience from his memory. "I'm sorry, girls, I need to go lie down."

Before I could ask him if he thought letting his defenses down by lying down was so smart, he offered me a hug and ran down the stairway, calling for us to meet him in the social room when we were done.

"That, there, is my hero," I laughed and Maddy joined me.

Hand in hand, we entered the fifth-floor ritual room by ourselves.

I knew that Poe's warnings were now manifesting into truths. And his overly imaginative self wasn't just being, well, overly imaginative. If both Chuck and I experienced something in the matter of a couple hours, there was definitely something here, but what, and why were we targeted?

The room was humongous. Carpeted, with rows of pews and seats on both sides of the room, a large chair stood at the foot of the room and the head of the room. In the center was an altar of sorts.

"Let's walk and see what we feel," Maddy suggested.

We walked the perimeter of the room until we came to one location right of the doorway out.

"The energy shifts," I said, "My head feels funny, much like it did in the basement."

Maddy nodded, her hazel eyes brighter than the flashlight that we were holding.

"It's a doorway, for sure," I jumped in and then out. A static electricity could be felt.

"I wouldn't do that if I was you," a voice from the entryway called out. One of the event organizers stepped into the room. "Chuck told me what happened and I thought I best check on you. I tried to call you on the walkie-talkie, but there wasn't any answer."

I lifted up the black device to see that it was on. I shined the flashlight on it, and held it up for him to see.

Doug hesitated for a moment. "Doesn't surprise me that you were blocked. This room has something negative attached to it," he informed us.

"What is it, Doug?" I inquired.

"Not sure, we just call him the shadow man. The other night our group investigated here and every single one walked in that spot," Doug pointed to the suspected portal. "And everybody blacked out."

"What?" I said, stunned and trying to stay objective.

"It's true. Everybody with the group is a first responder, too. We have no theories except for time travel, time continuum, or a portal of some sort."

"I have heard that quartz can generate energy. What is this building made out of?" Madelyn asked.

"Limestone. Actually most of Indiana is limestone. Native Americans were the first people to discover limestone in Indiana and not long after American settlers used the rock around their windows and doors and for memorials around the towns. The first quarry was started in 1827," Doug stated.

Both Madelyn and I studied crystals and stones and knew a bit about many. Ironically, we were going to be giving a lecture the next afternoon on crystals. Limestone is a sedimentary rock that usually forms in lakes, streams, rivers, and oceans. Most limestone is deposited in warm shallow seas. It is made up of many things such as shells, compacted crystalline rocks, plant and animal matter, and decaying algae. Limestone is a great source of fossils. Could it be that energy that signals paranormal activity by keeping the light energy out and the dark energy within?

"Buildings such as the National Cathedral, the Biltmore Estate in North Carolina, the Empire State Building, and the Pentagon feature Indiana limestone in their exteriors. And many churches use it within their interior," Madelyn added.

"And is the paranormal or portals attracted to limestone, or..."

"No, it is thought that they can't escape through limestone. They can move, but they cannot leave," Doug interrupted.

"And much like secrets, they stay hidden with the walls of the history within," I heard Poe say.

"So has anybody been possessed by whatever is here?" I asked, a bit frightened of the answer.

"Not that I am aware of. Thoughts attract things. If you have good thoughts, you bring good things. If you have negative thoughts, you bring negative things. Dark spirits feed off of fear. Like a lion that can sense it, so the dark can, too. We don't allow anybody to feed or taunt it."

Just as Doug finished his sentence, I felt as if someone reached from the darkness and scratched my left leg. I jumped back and yelped. Shining my flashlight on my calf, there was no mistaking the blood that was dripping down and staining my white sock.

"I need to find Chuck," I said, running to the stairwell and down the three flights of steps. I opened the door to the social room to find him sprawled out, snoring on a couch that looked to be about as old as I was. "The Lord is my shepherd; I shall not want. He maketh me to lie down in green pastures: he leadeth me beside the still waters. He restoreth my soul: he leadeth me in the paths of righteousness for his name's sake. Yea, though I walk through the valley of the shadow of death, I will fear no evil: for thou art with me; thy rod and thy staff they comfort me. Thou preparest a table before me in the presence of mine enemies: thou anointest my head with oil; my cup runneth over. Surely goodness and mercy shall follow me all the days of my life: and I will dwell in the house of the Lord forever." I whispered it three times as I sat in the chair next to Chuck, my hand softly resting on his arm. His eyes fluttered open.

"I was snoring, huh?"

I laughed and nodded. He was known in the paranormal communities for being the most annoying investigator, as more times than not he would find a quiet place and fall asleep. His snoring reverberated throughout wherever we were investigating and contaminated any recording evidence.

"Do you remember anything?" I asked.

Chuck sat up on the couch and smoothed his dark hair back before answering, "Hell yeah. Something tried to enter me. And I wasn't having anything to do with it either."

"Were you scared?"

"No, mad. I was really, really mad. Still am."

Chuck got up and stretched just as the door opened and the remaining teams walked in, along with Madelyn and Doug.

"I don't want to talk about it, though, Kristy," he whispered with a warning tone.

I nodded and gave Maddy a look and without words she understood. Chuck could be testy. Not sure who he reminded me of, I smirked, looking over at Poe who was standing over by the doorway looking concerned. Alto was next to him with his normal indifferent look on his face, but no indication that an exorcism would need to be performed.

It was 10:00 o'clock when we called it a night at the Freemasons Hall and walked to the hotel where we picked up our car. Mexican for dinner was the consensus, along with margaritas for Maddy, Chuck, and me. We steered away from any conversation that had anything to do with ghosts, demons, and the paranormal.

It was midnight before we were tucked in our bed at the hotel. I closed my eyes to try to sleep, but I was bothered and felt curious, and also feared the answers. My phone jingled and I looked over at Chuck, who already had his CPAP machine on and was fast asleep. I thought maybe it was Madelyn texting, or maybe the kids at home, so I climbed out of bed and padded to the desk that sat in the corner by the window where I had the phone charging for the night.

There wasn't any phone number or name listed on the phone, only one word. *Brotherhood*. I shook my head and looked to see if Poe was in the room, but it felt empty. My eyes felt droopy, so I climbed back into bed and fell asleep.

You say—"Can you hint to me what was the terrible evil which caused the irregularities so profoundly lamented?" Yes; I can do more than hint. This "evil" was the greatest which can befall a man. Six years ago, a wife, whom I loved as no man ever loved before, ruptured a blood-vessel in singing. Her life was despaired of. I took leave of her forever & underwent all the agonies of her death. She recovered partially and I again hoped. At the end of a year the vessel broke again—I went through precisely the same scene. Again in about a year afterward. Then again—again—again & even once again at varying intervals. Each time I felt all the agonies of her death—and at each accession of the disorder I loved her more dearly & clung to her life with more desperate pertinacity. But I am constitutionally sensitive—nervous in a very unusual degree. I became insane, with long intervals of horrible sanity. During these fits of absolute unconsciousness I drank, God only knows how often or how much. As a matter of course, my enemies referred the insanity to the drink rather than the drink to the insanity. I had, indeed, nearly abandoned all hope of a permanent cure when I found one in the death of my wife. This I can & do endure as becomes a man—it was the horrible

never-ending oscillation between hope & despair which I could not longer have endured without the total loss of reason. In the death of what was my life, then, I receive a new but—oh God! how melancholy an existence.
—Edgar Allan Poe's Letter to George Eveleth in 1848

Poe sat at his desk, tears falling and staining the parchment paper. I stood outside his front door and gazed into his window. I was almost surprised to see his tears were water and not blood. He reached down to pet a calico cat that rubbed affectionately against his right leg. Animals knew the sadness within the soul even when we denied the true emotion from bursting through. But Poe owned his emotion mostly through his writings. It was as if he was stuck riding in the boat in between two rivers; Acheron and Styx—woe and hate, without a means to move to a heaven. *Why was he so tortured that he couldn't stop grieving?* I contemplated. I, too, had lost—my first husband to another woman and my son to the military. I sighed louder than expected.

"Sara, I didn't notice you there," Poe said, opening the heavy wooden doorway.

Startled and a bit embarrassed at peering in without an invitation, I thrust my hands in the coat of my blue paisley dress. "Mr. Poe, I apologize. I went to knock, but noticed that you looked to be busy and thought I would try another time. I'll come back," I said, turning around.

"No, no, come in, Sara. What a welcome surprise. How is Edward?"

"Thank you, sir, for asking. He's been better, but I believe he's on the mend. His breathing is much more stable."

"Please don't call me *sir*, Sara. Edgar will do. If I recall, it was pneumonia that he's been fighting?"

I nodded.

"Edward is a good man, Sara. I know that you have been through romantic challenges just as I, and more than likely like thousands of others. It is apparent that Edward is quite taken by you."

I nodded. I did feel quite grateful. After my first husband abandoned me and his children, I wasn't quite sure what I would do, but then Edward found me and took my children in as his own.

"Congratulations to you, too, sir, I mean, Edgar. I heard of your engagement."

"Pfft," Poe motioned with his hand for me to sit down, "Yes, Sarah Whitman is a fine woman."

I sat down on the sofa. I couldn't help but grin. I wasn't convinced by his words that he was telling the truth, or at least the whole truth and they certainly didn't shine with love.

"But you, Sara, you already know all about that," Poe grinned back, running his hand through his dark hair.

I tucked an auburn curl back into my bun. I could once again feel a blush rise to my cheeks.

"Now shall we get to work?" Poe sat across from me in a wingback chair and held out his hands.

I smiled, closed my eyes, and took hold of both of his hands. With a deep breath, I began.

"Kristy!"

"Huh, what?" I mumbled, rubbing my eyes and looking around to see Chuck staring at me with one eyebrow raised.

We had gotten home from Indiana in the afternoon, and the weekend's adventure had exhausted me. I had laid down in front of the television just for a second, and looking at the clock on the mantel, it looked like a second had turned into three hours. I also felt even worse than when I first lay down.

"I'm sorry," I apologized to Chuck. "You should've woken me up earlier."

Chuck smiled and bent over to give me a quick peck on my lips. "No, it was completely fine. I would have let you sleep, but you were yelling in your sleep. I was worried."

The image of the completed dream flooded me at once. I was sitting in Poe's house. It was 1848. I knew that from the letter he was penning. And instead of me as Kristy, I was me as Sara. The same name I always felt was my soul name. The very name that my parents were tempted to change because Kristy never felt right.

"Sara, please be careful. They can't know what you know. What I know."

"Edgar, I fear for your life," I said softly.

"I've died several times over, Sara, I don't fear death. I fear living."

"Who is Reynolds?" I asked, squinting. "And why does he visit me in spirit so much with an apology for you?"

As soon as I took hold of Poe's hands, I received a horrific headache. I tried to wish the vision out of my head, but every time I glanced his way, the psychic visions and warnings intensified.

"My father. But he, like everyone else, has abandoned me or died. Or abandoned me into death"

"I . . . I don't understand," I stammered.

"My mother was a beautiful actress," Poe said, taking on a dreamy look. "She performed for the wealthy from far and wide. She made the mistake of falling in love with one such man from Virginia, near the North Carolina border. He would have nothing to do with her when she told him the news. He was a farmer and a merchant, and him and his lineage quite affluent. Although he was a nice man, he wouldn't take us in when my mother passed away."

"Us?" I saw a young girl in my vision and the story began to unfold before my eyes. "Your sister and you shared the same father, didn't you?"

Poe pursed his lips and sighed. "It was because of Reynolds that we were given what he thought would be good homes, instead of being shuffled off to orphanages, and yet I was an orphan still the same. I am certainly not angry with him. Although I often wish that my mother would have aborted me. I guess that is why I went to help Mary Rogers. She thought she was with child. She knew what a tormented life I lived with parental problems, and she wanted advice," Poe laughed and threw back his head. "Can you imagine, someone asking me what to do? I wish I had known you back then, Sara, I would have sent her to you."

"She wasn't pregnant, Edgar. She told us that during our last sitting. She was murdered. And you know exactly who it was who murdered her, and many others," I added. "You need to let the guilt go. Even if in a story of yours. Kill it, Edgar."

Poe affectionately reached out, hugged me, and dropped a few coins in my hand. "I would give you more if I had it, Sara."

I slid the welcomed coins into my pocket. I was saving for some fabric to make new dresses for the girls.

"Next week?" I asked.

"Yes, but let's choose another time. I am still afraid that you are being followed. Do you sense the same?"

"I will be careful. Until next week." I bent down to bid farewell to Poe's cat, then I walked through the door that he held open for me.

Without looking back, I quickly walked back to my home where my children and husband awaited my return. On the trip home, something white caught my eye. Lying on the grass, next to a graveyard was a large white feather. I bent over and picked it up. My heart stopped ever briefly. When I sensed death, I was given signs through found feathers. One feather was a year's time. More meant sooner. I swallowed hard and clenched the feather in my fist, tearing up the feather, pull after pull. But I couldn't make it go away.

Someone was going to die.

chapter ten

"Maybe you were right," I stammered.

I know nobody likes being wrong, but the Scorpio in me *really* hated being wrong.

Chuck grinned at me. "You might be the psychic medium, but I am pretty intuitive myself, pretty lady." Chuck sat down in the chair next to me and threw on a Detroit Red Wings baseball cap. "But, it all worked out. I'm not possessed. Or am I?" He widened his eyes and stuck out his tongue.

I couldn't even laugh. I honestly felt bad for putting us in the predicament in the first place. After all, Poe's rage should've been an indication that something was going to happen. It's like that person who touches the iron even after someone says to not touch the iron. I touched the iron, and I didn't just get burned, so did Chuck.

Chuck could sense my melancholy and my guides stood by feeling helpless, too, although they tried to convince me to not beat myself up too badly. "Let's go into Plymouth for some lunch and a drive," Chuck suggested.

Plymouth, Michigan, a quaint town just twenty miles west of Detroit, was first settled in 1825 and was greatly influenced by its New England counterpart. There was always something comforting to me about walking through the town. It helped to temporarily sooth a homesickness that I had from another time, another place. Although over the years Plymouth had become yuppified, with house prices some of the highest in the area and restaurants that lined the main street offered expensive dining options. We, however, often ate in an area of Plymouth that was a bit more blue-collared called Old Village.

George Starkweather was the first child born to settlers of Plymouth. He saw the potential of a railroad to the mostly farming and industrial community, that was thanks to Henry Ford, who built a mill there. It was George Starkweather who decided that the North Village of Plymouth would become the new center of town, so he built a new store on the corner of Liberty and Starkweather, near the railroad. Other business owners took heed and began building around him in the area that is presently known as "Old Village." Housed in the building that was George Starkweather's general store is *Hermann's Olde Town Grille*, one of our favorite hangouts.

In Michigan you never knew day-to-day if you would have to turn on your furnace or air conditioning, but this particular May day was in the low 70s and mostly sunny, so we decided to sit outside on the patio that ran parallel to Starkweather Street. After ordering our meals, we looked around at the houses that lined the street. Each one had its own unique architecture and was painted with bright and friendly colors. Many boasted large front porches and several of the neighbors sat and waved in greeting to passersby, strangers, and friends alike.

After a delicious lunch of margheritta pizza, barbecue chicken salad, and iced teas, we decided to take a stroll to my favorite house in the area. It was the house reminiscent of the one in Charleston that I fell to tears in front of. I could sense Poe walking with us. He also felt at home in this town and often urged me to move away from our 1950s brick ranch. But until he gave me the winning lottery numbers, we weren't going anywhere.

"Do houses hold energy?" Chuck asked, his head cockeyed.

We stood in the park that sat in front of the house that I sorely loved, even ached, to call ours.

"Absolutely," I said, nodding. "Houses, furniture, souls…"

"And do things miss like people do, or is it that people miss the energy from things?"

"I think both," I answered in what felt like a faraway voice.

I knew that I couldn't explain it, but I did believe that they did. I could pick up a piece of 1800s stoneware pottery and know that it belonged in my china cabinet in a house that I never owned in this era. Or look at a doll and become frightened because it reminded me of the doll my mother from another time had made as a remembrance for my sister who died from a disease that no longer existed.

"We have to go back to Baltimore, Chuck."

He looked at me once more with his head cocked, but this time the other way. "Okay, when?"

I looked over at Poe, who was leaning against an old oak tree and staring off into his own world, whether this one, a past one, or into the other side, I didn't know. He didn't give me any indication, but I knew that we had to go soon and didn't have any indication as to why.

"Soon. I will look at my schedule tonight and see what I can work out."

When we got back to the car, I turned my cell phone on to find a voice message from an out-of-state number. It wasn't abnormal for me to get strange calls. Several years ago I quit my corporate job to do life coaching, psychic mediumship sessions, and psychic detective work. Since then, there hadn't been one day when I looked back and regretted that decision. With the support of Chuck, the kids, and my guides, I never once thought that I couldn't do it, but there were some dicey times when I wondered if I would have any clients that week so that I could pay the bills. It only took me two years to build up a large clientele base, and a whole lot of hustling, and although I was grateful—instead of wondering if I would have clients, I wondered when I might be able to take time off as I was booked six months to a year out. Many times I forgot to cross myself out for holidays and birthdays, making the family threaten to take my calendar and choose my available days and times. It was a work in progress being an entrepreneur. And I loved every second of it.

I hit play on my voicemail:

> Kristy, my name is Brent. I am a private investigator for several families who have missing or unexplained murdered sons, brothers, and/or boyfriends. I received your name from an officer that you know. Could you give me a call when you have time to talk?

Chuck heard the message and looked over at me. "Call him," he softly urged.

I tried to unplug, but it was hard. I was learning, or trying to at least, but I had this constant urge to help others. Sometimes at the cost of losing myself.

I hit *call back* on the phone. I heard just one ring when Brent answered with an informal, "Hey, Kristy."

For the next twenty minutes he attempted to explain the cases. "Ever hear of the Midwest Killer?"

I used to read everything and anything about true crime cases, but my schedule didn't lend itself to do much reading and when it did, I picked up some inspirational nonfiction most of the time. The name sounded familiar, though, and I wondered if I had possibly heard it on a *60 Minutes* or *20/20* type show.

"In a nutshell, there are several young men, mostly college kids, who have gone missing. Some are still missing, others are found but almost always found in the water near where they went missing. There are several common denominators in these cases—they go missing from a bar, they are in a college town, they are men between the ages of seventeen and twenty-eight and many are thrown out of the bar for being intoxicated."

I tried to think back if I had read anything on the cases, and I wondered curiously if this wasn't related to a case that I took on with another private investigator back in 2006—the Brian Shaffer case. Brian had gone missing from a bar in Columbus, Ohio. On the night of Friday, March 31, 2006, Brian Shaffer, a twenty-seven-year-old, second-year medical student at Ohio State University went out with friends to have a few drinks and celebrate the beginning of spring break 2006. Around 9:30 p.m., the men headed to the Ugly Tuna Saloona, a bar located near the OSU campus. At 9:56 p.m., Brian called his girlfriend, Alexis, who at the time was visiting her family in Toledo, Ohio. He told her he loved her and that he would see her when she came back to Columbus. The two had planned on taking a vacation to Miami and were scheduled to leave for Florida on Monday, April 3. Shortly after talking to Alexis, Brian and his friend walked/barhopped until their final destination led them to the Ugly Tuna Saloona where they are seen in the surveillance tape at 1:15 a.m. The next time Brian is seen on camera, he was outside of the Ugly Tuna, at the top of the escalator, talking with two girls; he appears to say "bye" and turns toward the bar. He disappeared from the camera's view and has not been seen since. Despite a search I did with several connected to the case, the police refused to accept any psychic information that I received and to this date, Brian remains missing.

"The men are all determined by the cops and the medical examiner to have died accidently or by suicide. We don't believe this to be the case at all. Two retired New York City detectives coined these 'killers' after a cryptic calling card left behind at most all of the murder scenes. Whatever you call them, we believe we have a serial killer, or killers, on our hands." Brent took what sounded like a puff from a cigarette.

"Wait, why is it just a theory? If you see the same calling card at each scene, then there is no coincidence with that, right?" I thought about what Poe always told me—nothing is ever a coincidence.

"Police discount it as pure graffiti. And it is always different. Serial killers are often consistent. That is why this is so baffling. There is an awful lot of inconsistencies. And to be honest, I think because of that the police and the FBI are staying far away from this."

"And calling it an intoxicated college boy falling into the water is nice and clean."

"Exactly."

Chuck pretended to not be listening, but if he had antennae, they would have been high in the air.

I put my hand to my forehead and rubbed my brow, anticipating a headache. I hated disappointing anyone.

"Brent, I only work with the police on cases. It is a hard-and-fast rule that I adhere to since putting my life in jeopardy a few years ago."

It was true. I was like a psychic vigilante, assisting families of missing and murdered people, and I ended up having a killer chasing me. It sounded like a Lifetime movie, but it was my life. I honestly don't know if I would believe it if I wasn't living in it myself.

"Fair enough," Brent answered. "I can give the cops your name, but I highly doubt they will call. But, your friend told me that you have visions and feelings, right?"

"Uh-huh," I answered, already knowing where this was going. "Nighttime is a nightmare, no pun intended."

"Well, if you see, feel, or hear anything, do you mind passing it along to me? I have one kid that is missing and his parents are beside themselves. I am pretty sure he is in the river…"

This Brent was good. In the beginning of the conversation he explained that he was also a retired detective. Working for many detectives over the years I recognized their manipulative tendencies. It was rarely done in a vicious manner, but the theme was consistent—befriend and get information. Clean and cut.

Chuck whispered, "Throw the man a bone, Kristy."

I hushed Chuck and rolled my eyes. "Yeah, he's in the river. Not far from where he went missing. There is an abandoned house a block away that he was killed in—poisoned. He's stuck in some brush under the water, which is why the divers didn't find him. He'll float as soon as more boats get on the waterway and shake him loose."

I was beginning to not feel well and my head felt dizzy. No matter how many murder cases I saw, it never got easier. And I hoped it stayed that way. If I ever got to the point where I felt desensitized, I feared my abilities as a whole would do the same.

"And the killer, or killers, Kristy? Do you know who it is?"

I could almost feel Brent holding his breath. I only wish I had the answer to give him. It would be like a lottery ticket for him—not that he didn't care about his clients, but it was a job. Unfortunately I came up blank on the who. I could just see the where and the how. Two of the three wasn't so bad, right?

"Okay, well, thanks anyhow. If any of your spidey, or smiley, senses tells you more, I would really appreciate a call."

I agreed to call him if I saw anything and hung up just as we pulled into our driveway. What I weekend, I thought—secrets, scandals, portals, demons, killers, and past lives. Could it get any weirder? I looked over at Poe, who was intensely talking to Alto. Maybe weird was the new normal.

chapter eleven

"The dead will and can influence the living," Poe blurted out.

"And is there some sort of dead police that can help with this?" I sleepily asked. I was lying in bed and contemplating taking a sleep aid. I wasn't sure how much longer I could go without sleeping well. I think it had already been five straight days of nightmares and past life visions that seemed to possess my nighttime hours. "Oh, wait…Cheap Trick talks about the Dream Police in their one song. Maybe I am on to something!"

"Kristy, you aren't taking me seriously!" Poe scolded.

"You've never liked authority anyhow," I teased, "or organized groups. You hate being criticized, but often criticize. Am I missing anything?" I asked, sitting up and putting my hands on my hips pretending to be in disgust.

"Oh, but that is why I love your husband so much. He does remind me of myself."

I rolled my eyes. It was true. Chuck and Edgar could have probably been best of friends in the nineteenth century, except that I think that they were so similar that they would probably have a strong love-and-hate relationship. They both loved bucking the system and did anything and everything to avoid authoritative figures.

"Capricorns are difficult, and you aren't any different."

"What makes me a typical Capricorn?"

"Well, Caps often have difficult childhoods where they feel abandoned, sometimes physically or sometimes emotionally. Many times they move away from their family, more than likely in an attempt to get away from the misunderstandings and communication problems. But, through all that, Caps are good friends—that is if you let them control the friendship. Oh, and they are very intuitive."

Poe looked at me wide-eyed. "I thought you weren't an astrologer."

"I'm not. It's too mathematical for me and math hurts my head."

We both laughed, because he knew it was the truth.

"You *are* intuitive, Edgar, and you know it. I wonder if that is the reason why we have been connected together. Are you aware that your first and only novel, *The Narrative of Arthur Gordon Pym of Nantucket*, about a group of shipwrecked sailors who kill and cannibalize one of their crewmates, a man named Richard Parker, actually came true in 1884? Forty-six years after your book was published, a ship in real life sank and three of the survivors killed and cannibalized the fourth surviving member of the crew. The victim was a young man named Richard Parker. It just so happened to be the very name of the man who was in your novel who was met with the same demise. Interesting, huh?"

Poe looked at me curiously and smiled. "A coincidence, you think?"

I shook my head, thinking back to the previous night's vision with Poe.

In the 1830s and 1840s, many Americans worried that increased drinking was immoral and not only did it ruin the health of the drinker, but also disrupted families and created criminal activity. Not much different from the effects it has today. In order to reverse the effects it was having on society, an organization was founded called the Sons of Temperance.

According to the Sons of Temperance website, the Sons of Temperance was founded in 1842 in New York City by sixteen men and was the oldest of many temperance and total abstinence "secret societies" that existed in the United States in the nineteenth century. The group quickly grew in size, and secret handshakes, knocks, and passwords were introduced in order to keep out those merely there for the socialization and not to solve the real problem. The Sons of Temperance conducted extensive background checks on every single person initiated into the group.

As part of an initiation ceremony, every new member had to promise not to make, buy, sell, or use alcohol. The exact pledge being, "NO BROTHER SHALL MAKE, BUY, SELL, OR USE AS A BEVERAGE ANY SPIRI-TUOUS OR MALT LIQUORS WINE OR CIDER." Afterward an elaborate ceremony took place.

> *"Be thou an example in word, in conversation, in spirit, and in purity. Brother; guard against all impurity in thought, word, and deed. Banish every impure idea from your mind. Let no foul word pollute your lips; nor an impure action degrade the august majesty of your soul, made in the image of its Maker. Shun the impure; they are moral lepers; they poison the heart, and kill the soul with second death, from which there is no resurrection. Bear ever in your mind the words of this sacred Book: 'Blessed are the pure in heart, for they shall see God.'"*

It was dusk when Edgar Allan Poe, dressed in his typical black clothing, took my hand, as Sara, and quietly guided me to the back of the building.

"I will unlock the door for you, Sara. There is a room off of the main room where you won't be seen."

"And what exactly do you want me to do, Edgar?" I asked, my pulse racing. We had spoken in passing about doing this, but Poe often had elaborate schemes that he discussed and most never came to fruition. I figured this was another one.

"There is a killer, or killers, among us, Sara. See if you sense anything in there. I do, but I cannot tell whom it might be."

I nodded in understanding. It didn't always work that way and Poe knew that, but I was willing to help. For the past few years, Poe and I would meet and conduct séances. He came to me first because he wanted to speak to his wife and his mother. But during the sittings, it was apparent that I wasn't the only clairvoyant, Poe was too. Sometimes we saw things that happened in the future, sometimes things that happened in the past. For the last year we had been haunted by murders. These men would visit us during our sittings and discuss their gruesome last moments. When asked who their killer was, the response was always the same. "My brother." It took us awhile to realize that they didn't literally mean their flesh and blood, but someone else. At first Poe assumed it was a Mason, but when they refused to allow him to join, he grew furious. It came to him that perhaps it wasn't a Mason at all, but another group altogether.

I knew that he wanted to break a big story. He wanted his name known far and wide. He also knew that I did not want my name known at all. I was just a farmer's daughter and a lawyer's wife. But most of all I was a mother to my beautiful children and I was frightened. Not only was I petrified of being discovered to be a psychic, I felt as if I was caught up in something that I couldn't get out of. Whether ethics and justice, or just plain fear, I agreed to help, with Edward's permission.

Sensing my apprehension and fear, Poe lovingly stroked my left cheek with his glove. "I will not allow anything to happen to you, Sara. You know that. I've promised Edward the same. Now, I will meet you back here after the meeting," he instructed, fixing his coat collar up and leaving me to pray that I saw something.

The large room filled up quickly. The chatter of the men rang within the limestone walls, almost hurting my head. Or it was the energy that seemed to bounce throughout the hallways.

"Brothers!" a large man called out to the crowd. "Comrades," he yelled out even louder. The noise quieted. "We are ready."

The man rapped once.

Leader: When the crusaders of olden times went to war, they used their swords to kill their enemies. We use the sword also; not for the shedding of blood, but as a sign of warfare against Strong Drink, and an emblem of the law which is to destroy its great stronghold and headquarters: the Saloon.

Comrades, what is a Saloon?

Comrades: A place where alcoholic drinks are sold and where drunkards are made.

Leader: Is it a good or an evil place?

Comrades: It is evil always and everywhere.

Leader: How do we know that it is?

Comrades: A tree is known by its fruits.

Leader: What are the fruits of the Saloon?

Comrades: Drunkenness, vice, poverty, crime, disease, murder, death.

Leader: And what must we do to protect this from happening?

Comrades: Anything. Everything.

Leader: For how long?

Comrades: Forever.

Leader: Who are we?

Comrades: The Brotherhood.

chapter twelve

– March 2011 –

"I booked Gettysburg and Baltimore. Chuck, Micaela, Connor, and I will spend the Fourth of July in Fell's Point," I told Poe.

Poe clasped his hands together in excitement.

I knew that he just wanted us to go to Baltimore, but Gettysburg called to me after Chuck and my previous visit. I wasn't sure whether it was the history, the haunts, or still-unanswered questions on my past life journey when I originally began thinking of scheduling a Gettysburg trip. All I knew was that it was a location that I had to go to and I had to go in October. What better time to celebrate Chuck and my five-year wedding anniversary? Well, Chuck could think of a million different places, but he relented.

Before booking our room, I had asked several people where we should stay and Cashtown Inn was hands down the most recommended. When I asked why, I received the same "you won't be disappointed" reply. So I went online, looked at the photos of the rooms and chose the A. P. Hill room. I was completely unaware that several years before the room had been part of the *Ghost Hunters* episode where one of the stars, Grant, witnessed a frame moving in the middle of the night. I just chose it because it looked cute!

We also asked several people for recommendations on which tour to take and were given some vague responses, but a friend graciously loaned us several books that helped us get an idea as to what we wanted to do when we arrived.

Our seven-hour trip began by getting up at 4:00 in the morning with hopes of being on the road at 5:00 o'clock, but unfortunately that time was closer to 6:00 o'clock. As we made our way into Ohio, a rainbow appeared in the sky in front of us, and as we got into Pennsylvania, another rainbow appeared ahead. We took that as a positive sign. I was surprised that a main interstate didn't run through Gettysburg, but instead we had to take a two-lane road around the mountains to get into Cashtown. It was that trek that seemed to take the longest as we waited for tractors, horses, and even cows to cross the road, but we finally took the turn at Mr. Ed's Elephant Museum onto Old 30 to come into Cashtown, Pennsylvania, where the Cashtown Inn proudly stood.

On Mondays you have to check in between eleven and one, but we knew we would probably be later so I had called beforehand to let them know it would be closer to 3:00 o'clock, when in fact we got in just after one. No cars were in the lot and the door was locked so we followed the instructions that were left for us on the door as to where to locate our key. We unlocked the large front door and made our way to the steps when two ladies came out of the kitchen, surprising both of us. They instructed us on the following morning's breakfast and then they made their way out, leaving us to get settled and to unpack in our room.

The Cashtown Inn is about seven miles to the west of Gettysburg, Pennsylvania, but has its own history with the Civil War. Built in 1797, the name was created because the very first innkeeper would only accept cash for goods along the then toll road—a road that would serve as a supply line back to Virginia for the Confederate Army and bring the entire Confederate Army of Northern Virginia to Cashtown's doorstep at the very beginning of the Civil War. Oh, if those walls could talk. Or do they?

The paranormal activity began almost immediately, although I was completely unaware in the beginning what we were witnessing. Both Chuck and I could hear running up and down the stairs and just thought perhaps someone else had come in to the inn, only to open the door to our room and see absolutely nobody there and yet still hear the noises and creaking on the stairway as if someone were going up and down the third-floor stairs to the suites.

Our room, the A. P. Hill room, had a queen-size canopy bed, a beautiful replica Victorian vanity, and original dated signatures of visitors and stagecoach operators from the 1800s still visible on the walls. It overlooked the small town of Cashtown, the orchard, and the route the Confederate army took during the fateful battle. In a small frame, there was a note from Grant of Syfy's *Ghosts Hunters* that simply read: "Things move in this room." I laughed and thought it must be the many trucks that travel through the road, but that it was endearing.

Chuck and I had made the trip minus food, so we decided that lunch would be first on our agenda, and we quickly figured out that Lincoln Highway (Old 30) led to US Route 30. We both stopped breathing the moment the battlegrounds came into view—so much so that we pulled over and just stared at the vast land. Tears instantly sprang to my eyes. The energy was incredibly intense and so sad.

I saw Poe and Alto both overlooking the land. Poe's eyes clouded with emotion as he looked over at the battlefields.

I looked to see that Chuck had wandered off to grab a map from a small tourist building.

"There's speculation whether you would have gone to war or not, and if you had, whether or not you would've survived the brutality," I said to Poe.

Poe stood silent, still staring, as if watching the replay of the battle.

"Because, you're a lover not a fighter, right, Edgar?" I teased, trying to break the tension.

Before he could respond, Chuck asked me if I was ready.

Gathering control of my emotions, we continued down the road, quickly realizing that the road took us right into the town square that had a roundabout that was not only confusing, but defeated its purpose, as it was crazy congested with semitrucks. We did an eeny, meeny, miny, moe with regards to where to eat and chose the Pub and Restaurant. I found it so interesting when we entered and saw an article from the owner entitled "Believe." Since Poe came on the scene, he, Alto, and Tallie would show me the word *believe* as a sign that I was either in the right place at the right time, or that I needed to change my perspective to get to the right place at the right time. Glancing over the story, I couldn't help but smile. The owner had also overcome a lot in order to make that restaurant, her dream, become a reality. The food was just okay, but the wait staff was incredibly friendly and that evened it all out.

While we perused shops, we had come upon Cannonball Old Tyme Malt Shop and decided to stop in for a treat of an old-fashioned vanilla soda. We sipped our sodas as we wandered the streets, took pictures with Lincoln, and then decided to see if we could find Devil's Den and Sachs Bridge. Since we knew how to get to Sachs Bridge, we decided to stop there first. Night had fallen and time was of the essence.

Sachs Covered Bridge was built in 1852, and it was used by both Union and Confederate troops during the Battle of Gettysburg in 1863. Floodwaters swept it from its abutments on June 19, 1996. The bridge was rebuilt, and its trusses were supported with steel beams and raised three feet in elevation. Apparently the bridge was inadvertently turned the opposite way than it originally was when being repaired. Many paranormal investigators claim that the bridge is incredibly haunted by soldiers from both sides and I was anxious to see if it was all hype.

Both the bridge and the battlefields closed at 10:00 o'clock at night, and being a rule-keeper, I thought it best to adhere to the signs. As we pulled up to Sachs Bridge, we noticed a group hanging out at the bridge. The full moon reflected off the river, and I took a walk alone down to the bridge as Chuck stopped to take some photos. At the middle of the bridge, I felt as if I had gone through cobwebs, my sign that I was touching the veil to the other side. I began asking questions, looking around, and wondering why I couldn't see the spirits and could only feel them. It was something that I wasn't used to. I checked in with my guides.

"This is just the beginning," Alto warned. "Stay strong and learn."

I shrugged and allowed the feelings to come to me. It was then that I felt surrounded by at least ten entities who were a bit frustrated with their work being disturbed.

I walked back toward Chuck and asked him if he wanted to take the walk, but just as Chuck began walking, another car came up and three people got out. "Which end are the ghosts at?" a man asked me. I just laughed at him and continued shooting pictures. Chuck came back and shook his head as if trying to wipe off the excess energy and we made our way to the car just as three other vehicles drove in. I got in the passenger seat only to notice we had a hitchhiker looking at me from the outside.

"You must stay," I said. "You still have work to do, remember?" He merely nodded.

Chuck and I had a conversation before leaving on why nobody tried to cross over the spirits, as it seemed that there were both residual and intelligent entities. He laughed and asked if we could put a bounty on their head and threaten the ghost tour companies to pay up or else I would cross the soldiers over. He was just joking, I knew that.

We headed back to the inn as my phone and camera had died at Sachs and I wanted everything super charged. Plus, the temperatures were dipping down and I wasn't dressed for the weather.

After a quick super charge and super change, we stopped at a cemetery in Cashtown to check out some of the gravestones. Just as we turned into the battlefields, the sun began to make its descent and the fields took on a different feel. I was amazed at the amounts of people walking the fields and pathways alongside it, taking in the energy. We found ourselves at the Eternal Light Peace Memorial and got out to take a look. The moon was hung low in the sky as the sun set and we grabbed our cameras and recorders and made our way up the steps. Something caught my eye, and I saw a white-tailed rabbit hop right by me. Both Chuck and I felt a heavy energy overtake us at the same time and we noticed that we were completely alone on the grounds, or at least alive in this dimension.

We got back in the car and started our way through the entire route of battlefields, stopping and shooting pictures—and not where we felt activity, not where any book had told us was most active. We let the spirits guide us until we ended up at Little Round Top and then down to Devil's Den.

I could feel both Alto and Poe sitting in the back seat as Chuck and I rode around the battlefields. It was just before 9:00 o'clock at night and the sun had fallen, cascading shadows along the darkened battlefield, when Chuck stopped at an observation tower.

"Want to climb it with me?" Chuck asked.

"Not a chance," I laughed. Not only did I not like heights, I disliked heights in the dark.

Chuck parked the car, grabbed the camera, and, seeing that we didn't have a flashlight with us, used his cell phone as a light to maneuver himself to the top of a tower. I could hear his footsteps clang up the metal steps as I held my breath awaiting his return. With all of the car's windows rolled down, I could feel an energy shift and turned around to see if it was one of my guides, but they had both disappeared, probably back to the hotel to enjoy their evening. The energy grew thicker to the point I was ready to scream for Chuck to come back, but before I could yell, I heard his footsteps running faster and faster down the tower. He opened the door to the driver's side and stared at me with glassy eyes.

"Someone was up there with me," he said, panting and handing me the camera to put back in the case. "As I looked out over the battlefield, I could see soldiers, Kristy. I mean, I could see them! And then there was something, err, someone up there with me, and I was sure he was going to push me over."

I shuddered. The tower had a railing, but not one tall enough to save someone if they were pushed.

"Did you take photos?" I asked, hitting the menu button to scroll through, and noticing that he had. "Wait, look!"

I handed Chuck the camera to look at the photos that he had taken. On each photo he snapped there were several—what looked like people—soldiers illuminated in green, on the ground, standing up, kneeling. Some wore hats. Some looked to be holding guns.

"Are you certain there aren't real living people in the fields? Maybe there is a reenactment tonight," I reasoned, looking at the photos again.

Chuck shook his head and whispered, "No, nobody is out here but us. Presumably."

I knew that he was right, but I was still confused. Sure, I saw and even spoke to the dead, but there were several, maybe fifteen figures on the photographs. I wanted to make sense of it all and there wasn't any sense.

My entire life has evolved around the paranormal. If it didn't find me, I sought it. Lunch hours were frequently taken at the local historical cemetery where I would have peaceful conversations with those crossed over and ghosts-in-waiting. Not once during my excursions did I stomp and storm about forcing them to show themselves or demand they make lights flicker on my meters or force them to move a toy. Well, it did (and still does) help that I am a medium and can see, sense, hear, and communicate with those on the other side of life. Just as many, I have watched my fair share of paranormal shows. Some I love, some I tolerate, and then there are some that I just shake my head at in total disgust. Ghost hunting is normally as exciting as watching paint dry. I am also a proponent for respecting the spirits and ghosts as we live as one, under a different sky, a different paradigm, but still as one. So yelling and screaming in their home, at them, requesting them to do circus tricks that the family dog, if he could, would more than likely exchange some choice words after the request…well, it just doesn't cut it. It is disrespectful. Even snapping zillions of photographs, as if you are the paranormal paparazzi, is ridiculous.

I have found so-called haunted locations denoting on their contracts that it will not be allowed for anyone in a group to cross over a spirit. That they like their ghosts. I wonder if they would feel the same way if the tables were turned and they missed the last train to heaven. How they would feel being kept hostage? It is wise to think in paranormal situations as if the person is standing in front of you. Would you tell that person, "Sorry, I like the money that I am making off of you therefore you aren't allowed to leave to be with your family?" Although I have come into contact with some soulless people in my lifetime, I doubt that the majority would have the guts to say that.

As I glanced out at the battlefields, I curiously wondered why the soldiers hadn't found a way to Heaven, and thought perhaps they just needed a guide. Just as Alto, Tallie, and Poe guided me, maybe I needed to help guide them. I looked over at Chuck, who was staring straight ahead, obviously shaken, and thought it best to just go back to the hotel and sleep it off. Tomorrow was another day.

Although Chuck slept that night, I barely did. Before bed we had followed the directions in the room and put a quarter on a piece of paper and outlined it with a pen. The note on the desk said that the coin would move during the nighttime. I awoke in the middle of the night to a noise. Through the light from the street lamp peeking in the windows, I could see Poe sitting at the desk in front of the coin, playing with it. I grabbed my eyeglasses and looked at the alarm clock. The time, 3:33 a.m., glowed back at me. I shivered, not from the temperatures, but instead by the irony of the time. It is said that the three o'clock hour is witching time and ghosts and demons roam during the hour, wreaking havoc.

"What are you doing?" I whispered to Poe, glancing over to make sure Chuck was fast asleep. He was.

"There are ghosts here," Poe said, solemnly.

"Umm, no shit, Sherlock," I responded, smirking at him.

"Sherlock?"

"Forget it," I said, holding back my laughter and making a mental note to inform him of the impact his detective stories made on the literary world. Poe's work inspired Sir Arthur Conan Doyle and many others. Sherlock Holmes exists thanks to Poe, but now wasn't the time to tell him that.

"There are thousands of ghosts," he expanded. "I've never seen anything like it."

"Sad, isn't it? Can we help them?"

Poe looked at me as if he wasn't sure. "I'm sorry to wake you, Kristy. Go back to sleep."

I stretched and snuggled back under the covers and mumbled instructions for him to put the quarter back where it originally was and to not disturb the other two couples staying at the inn.

I fell asleep to Poe snickering, but woke a half hour later to the doorknob jiggling. I looked around but nobody was there.

"Chuck," I said urgently shaking his right shoulder. "Someone's trying to get in the room."

Chuck slowly opened his eyes and removed his CPAP mask. The doorknob continued to jiggle. Shrugging off the blankets, he quietly walked over to the door, unlatched the lock, and opened the door. I stood in back of him, peering around. In the hallway stood the four other guests, pajama clad and looking as confused as we were.

"What the...?" A young lady who looked to be in her late twenties asked, her brown eyes wide and her accent Southern.

We all looked at one another, confused, nobody know-ing how to begin until I blurted out, "Someone was trying to get into our room. Our doorknob was moving!"

"Ours too," the young lady said, introducing herself as Ann and her fiancé as Seth.

A heavy man with a gray receding hairline donning boxer shorts and a white T-shirt echoed the same. "I don't believe in this...ghost thing," he added as we all laughed. Because obviously this "ghost thing" had us hanging in the hallway at four in the morning, looking like the Scooby-Doo gang.

I looked around the hallway to see if Poe might be pranking us, but he was nowhere to be seen. Nor was any-body else, ghostlike or otherwise.

Morning came sooner than hoped, and I immediately scheduled a nap into our itinerary. As I jumped in the shower, I heard Chuck let out a hoop and a holler.

"The quarter moved!" he exclaimed.

I pretended to look as surprised and excited as he was, but I had to wonder if Poe had actually put it back where it belonged. After we were showered and dressed, we gath-ered in the Tavern for breakfast, meeting up with the rest of the inn's guests. As we chatted and laughed about our after-midnight hallway meeting, Jack, the owner of the inn, inquired what happened.

The older gentleman laughed and shook his head, still in amazement. "I came here for the history, not the haunts. I've never experienced anything like that until last night."

"Now that isn't true," his wife said, adding cream to her coffee. "We've heard cannons going off in the battle-field and heard the soldiers cry. He always thought it was recordings, but I knew it was otherworldly. And maybe now he's been convinced that I was right." She laughed and lovingly touching his arm.

"Yep, I think I believe now," he chuckled and took a swig of his black coffee.

The waitress brought the dishes of food out to us and the conversation quickly turned to which tour each of us had signed up for that day. Chuck and I decided to self-discover. I had gotten him to take the tours in Charles-ton, but that was pushing it, so we decided on a lazy day of exploring the town and battlefields, a definite nap, and then a ghost tour in the evening. Chuck was most excited about visiting Rita's, a small stand that sold Italian ice and custard, but became quickly disappointed when we drove by and it was closed for the season.

With several maps in hand, we made one of our first stops at the Wheatfields. On the humid afternoon of July 2, 1863, a wheatfield would become the center of fighting and death.

In 1863, the wheatfield was golden with ripened grain, but over the course of just one afternoon the field and the surrounding woods would be trampled and bloody, with the dead lying in the hot sun for days be-fore being collected.

We got out of the car and began to walk around the field, snapping pictures. I could feel both Alto and Poe, one on each side, as if I had bodyguards. As I walked, I immediately felt as if I had been shot in the stomach and I fell to the ground. The pain was intense and I wondered if it was true pain or empathy. I balled myself up on the sacred land.

My moans surprised Chuck, who ran over to me.

"What's wrong?"

"I've been shot," I answered with surprise. "I've been shot," I repeated, falling to the ground.

"Get in the car, Kristy!" he said, panicking.

"Kristy, get up and get in the car now," I heard Poe telepathically demand.

I sat up but still held my stomach. *Maybe it was something more,* I thought, but discounted that because I could feel the blood coming out of my phantom wound. "No, this is so cool. Who can say that they've been shot and not really have been sh—?"

Before I could finish my sentence, I heard the quick steps of a horse come up to me and then felt a stabbing sensation underneath my right arm, as if someone had spiked me with a sword.

"Now I've been stabbed," I said, falling back on the ground. "I'm dying." I wanted to laugh, but it hurt. Bad.

Chuck mumbled some swear words, picked me up off the field, and began to carry me to the car.

"Stop, stop," I protested, "I'm okay. Honest."

"Get in the damn car, Kristy," Chuck argued, placing me in the passenger seat.

I could see both Alto and Poe staring at me from where I had dropped. They shook their head as if to express an unrelenting frustration. I couldn't really blame them.

I visualized a rainfall of white light around me, washing away all the excess energy. After a few minutes, I began to feel the tension in my stomach release and the pain in my arm diminish.

Chuck didn't say anything, just shook his head at me and then started to laugh. "Honestly, Kristy."

I grinned back, "But how cool is it that I can say I was shot in Gettysburg?"

After all the excitement, we decided that it was the best time to get some lunch and go back to the inn for a nap. As we climbed the steps to our room, we were met at the landing by the younger couple holding their luggage.

"Checking out?" I asked, startled. They had told us at breakfast that they were going to stay one more night before heading home to Georgia.

Ann brushed her long, brown hair with her fingers and whispered, "Seth's scared. I am good with all of this— I grew up in Savannah—but he's freaked out."

We wished them a safe trip back home, but before we unlocked our room door, Seth called up to let us know that the other couple also checked out and informed us that according to Jack we were the lone guests there for the night.

It didn't faze me or Chuck. After all, my life was haunted, not just this town, and thankfully except for being shot on a battlefield, Chuck was used to the craziness that ensued.

The hour nap felt more like eight hours, and I was extremely grateful. As we dressed for dinner and the ghost tour, we heard footsteps in the hallway and assumed it was housecleaning, or perhaps a new guest. Opening the door to leave, we were met in the hallway by absolutely nobody. I grinned at Chuck, who mumbled something about wishing he had known what he was getting into when he married me. I laughed back at him, knowing that he knew exactly what he was getting involved in, albeit maybe not to the degree.

We visited Dobbin House Tavern, where we were led down into a candlelight basement. Wooden tables were staged close together without any privacy, but instead like one big family having dinner.

Dobbin was the oldest standing structure in Gettysburg, dating back to 1776. Originally, it was built as a home for Reverend Alexander Dobbin and his family. According to the Gettysburg Tour Center, Dobbin was an integral part of establishing the area, and was highly revered. Although unsubstantiated, the home was rumored to be the very first stop on the Underground Railroad north of the Mason-Dixon Line. During and after the Battle of Gettysburg, the house served as a temporary field hospital, as most all buildings were—churches, homes, etc.

Chuck wasn't impressed. In fact, Chuck was freaked out and kept saying he felt as if he was in a dungeon. Without natural lighting, and candles as the only means of illumination, our neighboring dining partners—two businessmen in for a conference—offered us their pocket flashlight and advice on what to order. Although the food was good, it wasn't great, and by the end of the meal, Chuck was near full into a panic attack. I couldn't even see my spirit guides as the place was so jam-packed that not even spirits or ghosts could've fit in with or without a reservation.

We stopped at the convenience store to pick up some pops—or *sodas* as they referred to them—to carry with us on the ghost tour. Checking in at the Gettysburg Ghost Tours, we both used the facilities. Chuck had taken his unopened Diet Mountain Dew in with him and realized that he forgot it, so he ran in to retrieve it only for it to be missing. The girls at the counter laughed at him and said that the ghosts must've taken it. He was more than upset, but not wanting to accuse them of stealing his pop, his mood turned dark and ornery. I was already pushing the limit with him for going on this tour.

"Kristy, you see ghosts and spirits, why do we need take a ghost tour? You could be giving the ghost tour," he grumbled to me as I urged him to run and get another Diet Dew in hopes it would soften his foul mood.

He was right about the tours, though. Both Chuck and I did give ghost tours in Michigan, so this felt a bit like work to him, too. I wanted to hear more haunted history and see the hot spots, and didn't have any expectations of seeing a ghost. We were to visit the Lincoln Cemetery, the Farnsworth House, the Grove, the haunted creekbed, the Rupp House Museum, the Dobbin

House, the Jennie Wade House, the haunted orphanage, and the Victorian Photography Studio.

We ended up being only two of three on the tour that evening, which made for more locations and more stories from our tour guide. The irony was that I picked up on the fact that our guide didn't believe and I called him out on it.

"Oh, I want to believe. I think that is why I do these tours. One day, I am hoping, I will see something."

Poe stood next to the tall man who appeared to be in his mid-twenties. I could almost picture him being a Civil War soldier himself. His stance was straight and his behavior very polite.

"Tell him his grandfather is proud he's a teacher," Poe instructed me.

"And over here," our guide pointed, "is a witness tree that many mediums claim has certain energy. It is called a witness tree because it witnessed the bloody battle and holds the residential energy within."

I held my hand against the tree and saw visions of the battle within my mind's eye. Pulling back quickly, I looked over at Chuck. Nighttime had fallen and we each carried flashlights, while our tour guide held a lantern. Chuck put his hand to the tree and pulled away just as I had.

"I don't believe in mediums," the guide said, "but I do feel something, a vibration I guess you would call it, when I touch it."

"Tell him," Chuck urged as I shushed him, but Poe was prodding too.

"Well, I *am* a medium," I said, blushing in the darkness. "And your grandpa wants me to tell you that he's proud that you are teaching. First grade, is it? He shows you holding a guitar..."

It was now time for the guide to blush. We were walking up a large hill toward another location, but he stopped in the middle of the street and stared at me. The lantern lit up his face, tears welling in his eyes. I could tell that his relationship with his grandfather had been one much like my own—unexplained and otherworldy.

"Thank you."

I nodded and we completed the tour without any more of his "If you believe..." commentary.

Both Chuck and I were thrilled to get back to the inn, take a shower, and go to bed. We noticed that we were the only car in the lot when we unlocked the front door.

Climbing the stairwell, the inn was dead quiet, but as we made our way into our room we heard a clinging noise on the third floor. The third floor of the inn housed several suites, one of which was where the original innkeepers, Mary Mickley, and her family, tried to hide when the Confederate Army invaded Cashtown. The other suite was a two-room suite to the rear of the inn situated atop of the area that was used as a field hospital after the Battle of Gettysburg when General Imboden was charged with evacuating the Confederate troops. I motioned to Chuck not to say anything as I climbed the steps to the third floor. The doors were open to the suites, but they were vacant. I felt someone behind me and swung around to see Poe standing there, looking grim. I turned back around to see at least twenty soldiers that seemed to be caught within a loop of time. Various limbs were stacked up by the windows. Blood stained the walls and the floorboards. There was some movement among what I thought were corpses, but I couldn't tell if I was seeing their spirits or physical movement. Another noise startled me and I turned around to see Chuck looking around me, as if trying to figure out what I was staring at.

"Looks like we are it," I said, shivering at the vision from my memory. I glanced back up and everything looked to be back to normal.

After our showers, Chuck went to climb into the side of the bed he had slept in the previous night.

"Nuh-uh. I claim that side. If it's going to open the door, it's going to get you!" I joked.

Chuck shrugged, laid down, gave me a good-night kiss, and was fast asleep. Me, on the hand laid down, stared at the lace canopy, and listened. I swore I could hear something on the third floor, something dragging. I didn't want to remember what I saw, so I brushed it off and envisioned happy things like unicorns and fairies until slumber stole me, too.

It was only an hour later when I was startled awake by a loud thump. Chuck's breathing was still heavy. I grabbed for my glasses that were on the nightstand, but they weren't where I had set them before going to bed. I sat up, squinting hard and feeling all around the table, however they for sure weren't there at all. I sighed, deciding that I should use the facilities and go back to sleep. I would find my glasses in the morning, and the thump was probably in my dream. As I walked back to the bed, careful to walk around the bench that sat at the foot of the bed, Poe sat once more by the carefully placed quarter.

"On the mantel."

"What?" asking him, thoroughly confused.

"Your glasses are on the mantel," he said, not looking up at me.

Puzzled, I walked to the mantel, which was nearest my side of the bed, and sure enough my glasses sat there. I knew that I hadn't placed them there and looked at Poe for an answer, only to receive a shake of the head.

I put the glasses back on the nightstand, climbed into bed under the covers, snuggled up to Chuck, and was just about ready to fall asleep when the doorknob began to jiggle again. As if something out of the movies, an entity of a soldier walked through the door and past the bathroom door, its movement making the door slam. I lay there, unable to move. He walked to my side of the bed and sat down next to me on the bed.

I didn't know whether to scream, wake Chuck, or just plain run, but I was too terrified to do anything but stare.

"Ma'am," he started.

He sees me, I thought. I could see him, he could see me…where was Poe? I looked around to see him standing against the bathroom door and looking agitated.

I nodded back at him, noticing that I was shaking.

"My name is Nathanial Thomas."

His left arm had been cruelly sawed off and just a stump, bloody and oozing infection, hung.

"Do you know that you are dead, Nathanial?" I asked, looking at his uniform. He had a bloodied white under-shirt on with a wool blue coat swung over him. Dirtied and ripped sky blue pants covered his legs. He wore no hat, nor did he have a gun. He looked all of seventeen or eighteen.

Nathanial nodded, "But there is still a battle being fought, ma'am. I will not leave my post."

"What do you mean?" I whispered.

He didn't answer me, only looked at me with sadness in his eyes. "You remind me of my ma."

He went on to tell me his family story and how he died on the first day of fighting.

"Don't you want to be with your family?" I asked.

"I do," he said, "But there is still a battle being fought, ma'am. I will not leave my post," he repeated.

Then he disappeared, leaving me with what sounded like bodies being dragged down the steps. I yelped loudly and jumped on top of Chuck, waking him. I tried to tell him what happened, but I shook like a leaf, my soul feeling chilled and my mind horrified at what I had just seen.

Morning couldn't come quick enough. We hurriedly ate our breakfast when Jack asked us how our night had been. Not wanting to expand on anything, I just told him about hearing what sounded like bodies being dragged down the steps. He smiled and reminded us that we were the only guests that night. And then he said it was a common complaint, after all the Cashtown Inn was a field hospital.

Limbs would be thrown out the window after the amputations, but they piled up to the second floor there were so many. Horrified screams still echo as there was no anesthesia or pain medication. I was never so glad to get back home.

And yet Gettysburg called for me to come back. This time with the kids.

chapter thirteen

– July 2012 –

The kids begged that we not stay at the Cashtown Inn. After my stories, they weren't thrilled at the ideas of amputated limbs and bloodied soldiers, especially seeing that I was booking a suite.

So instead we checked into the Battlefield B & B, an 1809 farmhouse that stood on a beautiful 30-acre nature reserve. Just as in most all of the buildings that existed during the Battle of Gettysburg, this land had also seen its own share of fighting as it was smack dab on battleground and had been a field hospital. Union Cavalry officers had even stayed there on the night of July 3, 1863.

The farmhouse took our breath away as we drove up to it and the scent of baking oatmeal cookies did us in as we entered. We received a tour where it was noted that eight guest rooms shared the 1809 Civil War farmhouse and we were delighted to see that we were in the old part of the farmhouse, on the top floor, in General Merritt's Suite. The one room had a king-size bed, while the other a double, and then we shared a bathroom. Connor and Micaela moaned about sharing a bed, but it was only for a couple nights and then we would make our way to Baltimore. After unpacking, we went downstairs, grabbed some fresh, out-of-the-oven cookies and cups of lemonade, and explored the trails. The kids ran ahead, while Chuck and I leisurely spent our time looking at the beautiful wildflowers and the many birds, butterflies, and squirrels that we came upon.

Just as we rounded the corner where a lily pond was, my cell phone rang. Chuck's eyes squinted a warning, but I saw from the phone number that it was the private investigator and excused myself to the back porch.

Without even saying a hello, I knew. "Another one, Brent?"

"Yeah, it is the holiday week, after all," he confirmed.

I sat down on the step and found Poe looking back at me, curiously.

"Did he go missing from a bar like the others?"

"Just disappeared into thin air like most all of them do."

I could hear the frustration in his voice. Before I spoke, I checked in with Poe who nodded in agreement. "I wish I knew who it was, but I think I have more information for you. I'm on vacation with the family. Can I send it over to you when I get back?"

"Anything you have, Kristy, will help. Oh, and I am not sure if you followed the story, but the previous case we talked about, well his body was discovered floating in the river just as you said it would."

We said our goodbyes and I looked back over at Poe, who was now in his element petting five kittens.

"If these murders are connected to past lives, or to past promises…well, how does that work?"

"If you look at an old painting, underneath the painting there might be older versions of the drawing that were painted over. The surface painting is the present one, the others are there, just never seen, but they're part of the process. Those layers don't take away from anything, but the original painting is aware that it is there. It is all connected," Poe explained.

"When we reincarnate we keep a piece of our soul. And that soul continues to hold past memories, past experiences, but many times it is locked away. Do I have that right?"

"Just as with your gifts, they seeped through from the past to the present. You can ignore it, but you do a disservice to the quality of the present painting. The beauty somehow deteriorates if you don't acknowledge the entire process."

"Poe, why didn't you reincarnate?" I asked him, honestly curious.

"Who's to say that I haven't?" he chuckled, continuing to pet the kittens that were now crawling in my lap. "The soul can split in many pieces, Kristy."

I heard a horse neigh and the crumble of gravel underneath the tires of another guest's car and knew that our conversation was over. Plus I saw Micaela, Connor, and Chuck walking toward me. It was probably time for dinner and some battlefield exploring.

Connor had previously panicked when he saw sparse farmland, especially when wheat was growing. I was both curious and concerned as to what his reaction to the Gettysburg battlefields would be. From a young age, Connor showed a militant characteristic. His clothes had to be folded just so, his shoes cleaned just so, and his room in immaculate condition. His sister, on the other hand, was the opposite. At the age of two, Connor began going into Micaela's room and straightening it, as it drove him crazy for anything to be out of place. Now at sixteen years old he is still very organized and tidy, and Micaela is very messy. As the four of us got out near Culp's Hill, the scent of death took over the air, and we held our breath and grabbed our stomachs. The stench was so strong that we were overcome with an urge to vomit. We looked around at the other tourists, all of which had a similar response, and felt relieved that it wasn't just a personal experience.

The day lasted longer in July than during our previous October trip, but we were sleepy nonetheless. The four of us settled into the main bedroom and talked about our day and the plans for the next day when we heard a steady musical banging. Looking around and outside we saw nothing but the fireflies lighting the sky.

Connor swore he saw a young boy in the woods who darted as soon as he caught sight of him, but we were all too chicken to venture off into the woods at nighttime, flashlight or not.

Back in the room, the drumming began once again, so I perused a guest book for the room that "complained" of the same. Some noted that it was the air conditioning unit, while others called it the haunting of the Drummer Boy who had perished on that very land. No matter what it was, I hoped that it didn't keep up all night long. Thankfully it didn't.

"Mom!" I heard screamed from the next room.

Grabbing my glasses, I quickly, but carefully so not to fall down the steps, walked to the kids' room. There, Connor and Micaela sat up in bed pointing to a doorway in front of their bed. We had noticed it before they went to sleep and tried to open it, but it was locked and it was assumed to be a door to the attic.

"A soldier woke me up. He stood right there, Mom," Connor claimed. He went on to describe the ghost's attire, his hair color, and even what his boots looked like. Thankfully, he had all of his limbs. "I grabbed my own glasses to make sure that I wasn't dreaming. He was still there when I put them on."

"Cool?" I asked in question.

Micaela shook her head and responded, "Not so cool."

"Want me to sleep here or you in there?" I murmured, feeling tired and wondering what time it was.

"Nah, we will be okay. It can't hurt us," Connor reasoned logically. Micaela didn't look as convinced, but she stayed put.

After using the washroom, the drumming began again and I just laughed. I *was* paying for the experience.

The next morning's breakfast was nothing short of amazing. Everything was home cooked. The eggs were farm fresh, the orange juice was freshly squeezed, and the scones were warm out of the oven. After breakfast we were gifted with an amazing history presentation that kept all of our attention, and afterward the kids and Chuck shot a real musket—that was after the owners made sure to put the kittens away so they didn't scare. We had one more day of exploring and then were off to Baltimore. I was nervous and apprehensive, hoping that I would be able to put some missing pieces to the puzzle of Edgar Allan Poe. Chuck finally got to indulge in his Rita's Italian Ice and was happy that I didn't have an encore presentation in the Wheatfields, albeit I wasn't.

That evening was another ghost tour, this time with a different company as Chuck was still sore about his stolen pop. Although Micaela wasn't thrilled with going, she trudged with us like a trooper. We all had varying experiences along the route, and the tour guide even stayed with us afterward to explore some woods by the battlefield.

"Stay real quiet and turn off your flashlights," she instructed. "And then wait."

Trying hard to not make a noise as mosquito bit, it was maybe only a minute when we witnessed several soldiers, all holding lanterns, run fast through the woods right past us. I looked at everybody to see if they saw what I did and their faces confirmed that they had. It was normally only me who saw the physical features of a ghost or spirit and I oddly felt comforted in having the camaraderie.

Exhaustion and darkness blanketed us as we made our way back to the B & B. Well after midnight, we quietly crept up in and up the stairwell. We said our good nights and prayed for serenity. Neither the Drummer Boy nor the soldier appeared in the suite, which gave us a much more sound sleep. We awakened once more to a fabulous breakfast of homemade biscuits and sausage gravy. And again, another historical presentation, before we made our way to Fell's Point, but first we paid our respects to the soldiers in the battlefields.

The kids, Chuck, and I were sad to leave Gettysburg. I felt a bit empty, as if I hadn't discovered all that I had hoped. I tried to explain to Poe that it wasn't all about him, but he didn't agree. He was eager to get to Baltimore. So we reluctantly checked out and began another adventure. Maryland bound.

Poe's excited energy kept draining my phone. It was only a couple hours before we checked into the Admiral Fell Inn in the historic Fell's Point, but beforehand we stopped at Poe's House. The row house that Poe stayed at for many years is now a museum. A police car waited across the street as we looked at where to park. Poe whispered in my ear that our car was going to be stolen and that it wasn't important to see the museum. I was really disappointed in not going in, but I didn't really want the hassle of a stolen car. The neighborhood lent a lot to be desired.

Fell's Point was a bustling port in the early 1900s, but the surrounding neighborhood was filled with unsavory characters and businesses, such as warehouses, saloons, and brothels, that catered to them. In the center of the city was the Anchorage, built in late 1900, and was a boarding house for seamen to find a safe and Christian refuge. The mission was to encourage the traveling men to join a church and stay in a comfortable, safe boarding house, while staying away from alcohol. The Anchorage was turned into what is now the Admiral Fell Inn, what would be our home for the next few days. I found it ironic, if not coincidental, that the historic mission for the Anchorage had a very close likeness to the Sons of Temperance, and that it was steps from where Poe was last seen alive.

Attached to the hotel was a small bar called the Horse You Came In On Saloon. Noted as the very last place Edgar Allan Poe was seen alive, I decided to make that our lunchtime stop.

"Can I get you a beer?" our bartender asked as we sat down at a high-top table. A guitarist was setting up in the corner and the kids gave me a look as if to say *why are you bringing us to a bar?*

"She's a Poe fan," Chuck told the twenty-something guy. I laughed because if he only knew.

"Oh, so you will want a Poe!" he exclaimed and explained that it was their signature drink—the last drink Poe himself had, or so they spouted.

I glanced to see if Poe was with us, and he was, but at the end of the narrow bar by the back. He snickered at the memorabilia—photos and T-shirts that sported his mug.

"No thanks, I don't drink, but I would love an iced tea."

We ordered and enjoyed the music while we waited for our food. I saw Poe wandering around the small saloon. A group of young women sat at the table next to us and Poe sat next to a pretty blond until she jumped and hollered that a bug must've been crawling on her leg.

I was laughing so hard that I had to excuse myself to the washroom. As I exited, the bartender asked me if I wanted to hear some stories. So, I sat down at the end of the bar and he asked me if I believed in ghosts. I tried once more to hold back a giggle and just nodded and said that I did. Feeling comforted, he went on to share several stories.

"Even in death, Edgar is known to be a trouble-maker. The chandelier swings by itself and the cash register opens and closes as if it has a life of its own. I have had employees who have denied that Edgar's ghost exists or tease that they will never believe only for moments later the bar stool pulled out from under them or a glass to be pushed out of their hand. I can't tell you how many beer bottles have just dropped to the floor."

"Does it frighten you?" I asked him, looking over at Poe and wondering if he was playing ghost at his old stomping grounds when he wasn't around me. He just grinned wide.

"We make sure to say hello to Edgar when we come in and good night to Edgar when we leave. It's his place, he has made that known."

I nodded and was happy to hear that they were respecting the history and the haunts.

"What do you think he died from?" I asked, curious as to what the locals believed.

"Murder."

"Really? Didn't he die from rabies or from that alcohol over there," I pointed, trying to sound impartial.

The bartender shook his head. "That might be what the history books say, but without a doubt I believe that he was murdered. Oh, your food is ready," he said, smiling at me as if relieved to have a confidant.

"Well, did you see him?" Chuck asked me.

"Who?" I asked, still playing the fool.

"Edgar Allan Poe. Did you see him?"

"Nah, probably just a ghost story to get people in the door," I smiled and ate my lunch.

After a delicious lunch, great music that even had Connor tapping his foot, and a happy and content feeling, we headed to Westminster Hall.

Chuck, the kids, and I stood looking at Edgar Allan Poe's gravestone. It wasn't as hot as it had been during our previous visit, but the energy seemed different within the city. Instead of the hustle and bustle, the streets were vacant, making us feel unnerved. Chuck once more took some pennies from his pocket and handed them to us all to pay our respects.

I thought back to a report that I read several years back in 2009 when hundreds of people attended Edgar Allan

Poe's funeral to celebrate the two hundredth anniversary of his birth.

"You're dead again with a funeral revisited," I had teased Poe. "What will you wear to your own funeral?"

Poe's cousin, Neilson Poe, had never announced his death publicly and so fewer than ten people attended his service. And just as in his life, his death caused drama. Poe's tombstone was destroyed before it could be installed when a train derailed and crashed into a stonecutter's yard. Then Rufus Wilmot Griswold, a vocal enemy of Poe's, published a libelous obituary that damaged Poe's reputation for decades. And maybe to this day still does.

Poe had already been dug up once in 1875, and I thought how appropriate since he wasn't at rest during his life, and certainly not after his death. This time, however, they created a mannequin of a corpse to look like Poe and laid him in state at the old house. A procession on a horse-drawn carriage carried him through the town of Baltimore. With bagpipes playing and church bells ringing, participants wore period and modern clothing and listened to eulogies from various actors for his long-awaited funeral. Unfortunately ironic, an actor playing Rufus Wilmot Griswold read the scathing obituary to the crowd, continuing to remind all how well sensationalized his life was and still is.

Somberly, we all stepped away from the graveyard and silently drove back to Fell's Point for a nap.

It didn't take long for me to slip into sleep, if not mere minutes that ticked by like a stopwatch, and a familiar darkness crept around me once more, but this time it felt heavier.

"We are leaving for Charleston in the morning, Edgar," I said with tears springing to my eyes. "Edward has found a position that he will be quite happy with. And I do love Charleston much more than Philadelphia, albeit Edward isn't sure. I hope that he isn't doing this to appease me."

Poe nodded and took my hand, "Charleston. That is where we first met, Sara. Ah, how I remember being so spry," he laughed. "Edward is a lucky man."

I smiled at Poe. He was always quite complimentary and innocently flirtatious.

"What will you do now?" I asked. "About the Brotherhood?"

"I have a plan in the making as we speak." Poe looked around to see if anyone was in earshot. Nobody was, so he continued. "For exposure of the killers, I will assist with the slaves."

I gasped.

Recognizing that I was misunderstanding him, Poe continued. "I am not selling slaves, Sara. I am saving them. I have the intention of sneaking several slaves on the train with me from Baltimore to New York and from there to an abolitionist's home. I'm the least likely candidate to be looked at," he said, puffing his chest out.

I sighed with relief, however something still felt off to me. "Please be careful," I cautioned.

"There are some secrets which do not permit themselves to be told, Sara. They must be discovered. Look," Poe said, leaning over and picking up five black bird feathers. "Someone got into a fight, now didn't they, Sara? I wonder who won?"

I paled.

"I will visit you, Sara," Poe promised, offering me a farewell hug.

"I believe you will, Edgar," I murmured.

The nap left me feeling unnerved and on edge so when the kids and Chuck decided to go to the convenience store across the street, I decided to wait instead by the bar.

"Please be careful," Chuck cautioned. "This area is a bit shady."

The fireworks were going to be over the harbor and crowds were already beginning to form, along with street performers. I wished for a peaceful place where I could connect with Poe, but I knew that wouldn't happen. Standing against the brick wall, I telepathically called for him, but he was already standing next to me.

"Movies depict that you were found on a park bench."

His laughter rang in my head, "If only so lucky," he smirked.

"I'm here now, Poe. Help me help you..."

"I was going to expose the Brotherhood. The murders of young men were happening more and more frequently, but it was being attributed to alcoholism and accidents. The brutality of the murders weren't seen. Not like the Jack the Ripper killings. Their throats weren't slit. Their necks not choked. Instead, they were poisoned and dropped in a local river, harbor, or whatever waterway there was."

"The Sons of Temperance promise!" I exclaimed, thinking back to the meeting that I saw in my dream.

Poe smirked and nodded.

"Pinkerton was going to help me in exchange for help with a group of slaves in Baltimore that needed refuge."

"So you didn't miss your train?" I jested.

Poe rolled his eyes, "No," he flatly said.

"So you were found out or Pinkerton's group snitched on you? Were you double-crossed?"

Poe sighed, "I don't believe that Pinkerton's group had anything to do with it, but I did wonder."

"So you went to the bar…"

"I did. And I admit that I had a drink. I was an anxious mess. I didn't want to get married, I mainly just wanted to be free to write and marriage offered me that. So before our evening meeting, I ordered a drink. I thought that I would blend in with my outfit."

"You thought you were undercover," I laughed. "I don't think you realize how famous, or infamous, you were then."

Poe shrugged, "Regardless, it did me in. I saw a man in the back of the bar looking over at me and I thought nothing of it. Until later when I realized it was the same man…"

"At Loss's Tavern," I finished for him.

"I already had my drink, but the bartender must've poisoned me with some concoction. He probably thought

I would die instantly, but it took several days. Thus the story of my life—pain and agony."

Now it was my time to roll my eyes at Poe.

"And now the Brotherhood continues…"

The answered questions of Edgar Allan Poe's death didn't help me put anything to rest, because he was correct, the Brotherhood continued.

The man rapped once.

Leader: When the crusaders of olden times went to war, they used their swords to kill their enemies. We use the sword also; not for the shedding of blood, but as a sign of warfare against Strong Drink, and an emblem of the law which is to destroy its great stronghold and headquarters: the Saloon. Comrades, what is a Saloon?

Comrades: A place where alcoholic drinks are sold and where drunkards are made.

Leader: Is it a good or an evil place?

Comrades: It is evil always and everywhere.

Leader: How do we know that it is?

Comrades: A tree is known by its fruits.

Leader: What are the fruits of the Saloon?

Comrades: Drunkenness, vice, poverty, crime, disease, murder, death.

Leader: And what must we do to protect this from happening?

Comrades: Anything. Everything.

Leader: For how long?

Comrades: Forever.

Leader: Who are we?
Comrades: The Brotherhood.

The fireworks over the harbor that evening were a beautiful sight for a day of cruel awakening. On the rooftop of the Admiral Fell Inn, I held the hand of my husband and watched my two wonderful children as Fell's Point, Baltimore, became a happy memory through so much pain and horror that stayed within the tapestry of the past.

Epilogue

Edgar Allan Poe kept his promise. He continued to visit, but not in the way he believed it to be. Feathers continue to be my sign of death and I still follow his advice that there is nothing coincidental, just synchronicity, the drawings peeking through the painting of our lives, hinting at our purpose.

Poe continues to be an armchair detective, but working through me on various missing persons cases and murder cases with hopes of bringing justice. His passion, however, is aimed specifically with plans to one day expose the Brotherhood for who they are and to help fulfill the work that him and I, as Sara, had tirelessly spent hours working on. With his research and dedication and my channeling and ability to receive information with a husband who was then in the political and legal field, he hasn't let go of the ability to show the truth.

The killings continue today. The vow made over 160 years ago is still kept. Not by one, but by many. Some believe that the killer, or killers, are truck drivers. Others believe that they may be police officers or bartenders. No matter who the killers are, they are killers nonetheless.

The killers are monsters of the past who continue to kill innocent men, mostly men in their late teens to late twenties, college men. They always die under mysterious circumstances and are found in water. Police have been baffled in over a dozen states. Private detectives are hired, but find deadends and are just as confused by the who or why. Motives vary, as does the opinions of law enforcement with a hesitation of calling this the work of a serial killer. But with many dead, spanning hundreds of year, we know that the Brotherhood's pact is kept even today.

"There are moments when even to the sober eye of reason, the world of our sad humanity may assume the semblance of Hell." —Edgar Allan Poe

Just as the Gettysburg soldier hasn't left his post, Edgar Allan Poe remains dedicated to exposing evil and fighting the battle for truth. Forevermore.

Featherless Wings
Kristy Robinett

Within a moment of time, stilled
Giggling clouds dance to the sun
Uttering secrets in which to be fulfilled
Winds whisper promises to be done
Droplets of water begin to descend
Solitary refuge, folded wings
So frightened of the unknown, awaiting the end
But they look on, confident in what it will all bring
Sheltered in the violet haze
Shadows from the storm flitter about
The clouds move on and the sun beams down its rays
Shaking his wings, slowly, of all his doubt
He begins his flight, wavering in the breeze
Ever radiant, in all his splendor
Weaving in and out with a tease
Fate about to surrender
Into the waning dusk, they watch him soar
His wings melodically flutter in dance
Destiny ahead, beckoning more
Featherless wings, embracing the chance

Connecting with Your Guides

Spirit guides can help you accomplish and achieve success in every area of your life by gently and consistently guiding and nudging you along your soul journey. Because we all have free will and free choice, you can decide to go against the current, and that is when your guides can call on others in the spirit world to give you resources in the way of people and finances, insight and love. We, however, have to be open and willing to accept it. Once there is recognition of assistance, even if there isn't an awareness of who it is coming from, then doors can and will open wide.

Spirit guides show us they are around in many different ways.

1. **Sending signs and symbols**. Every single day we receive signs and symbols from our spirit guides. It might be that butterfly that won't leave you alone, or the driver in the car that is going super slow in front of you. The most important thing to realize,

though, is that everything that happens in our life has a meaning or reason behind it. If your eye is twitching, what aren't you seeing? Or if your basement flooded, what part of your life feels like it is collapsing? If you lost your wedding ring, what is the meaning behind that?

These signs and symbols, which seem to be random, have deep meaning. Spending time interpreting the signs and symbols according to what is happening in your life to understand them at that moment will help you live a more intuitive life.

2. **They yell.** Yes, they even yell at us. Have you ever heard your name being called out just as you were falling asleep? That is your guides trying to get your attention. Most of the time it works, it is just not understood who it is and what they want unless you begin working with your guides on a consistent basis.

3. **They show themselves.** If you have ever seen a shadow out of the corner of your eye, don't call Ghostbusters, it's more than likely a guide watching over you.

4. **Gut feelings or intuitive thoughts.** You might wake up one morning and just know that you need to take a different route to work, but you don't know why. That is a guide whispering and nudging you. It could have been protecting you from an accident

if you had gone that way. Some people may believe that when they sense danger it is a coincidence or give credit to a deceased loved one, when in fact it is a spirit guide who is assisting in their safety.

5. **Sending people into your life**. Your guides actually conspire with other people's guides and create meetings or encounters that to you may feel are just a chance encounter, but in fact they are carefully schemed.

Everybody has the ability to connect with their spirit guides and in return stay more intuitively connected with one's own life and the life of loved ones around. It just takes time and practice to be able to hear, see, and/or feel your guides.

1. **Notice the signs and symbols**. Nothing in our lives are ever random. Take notice when the same sequence of numbers comes up. Or when a bird pecks on at your window. Or when so-called coincidences continue to happen, making you wonder if they were coincidences at all.

2. **Pay attention to the people being sent into your life**. People are sent into our lives for several reasons, even if it is a painful lesson. Pay attention to those you meet. Maybe you keep meeting someone named Jason and you cannot figure out why

and discount it as strange, when in fact your guide is trying to possibly tell you his name. Or you meet someone who you feel a connection to and then cannot locate them again. It could be in fact your guide in human form.

3. **Listen.** When you hear your name being called, and yet nobody is there or they say they never said your name, listen closely, as there is probably a deeper message being shared. Or you might turn on the radio to hear a song, and then step into a store and hear the same song, and then back into the car to hear the exact same song. Listen to the lyrics. Listen to the message.

4. **Look.** You are watching television and all of a sudden, out of the corner of your eye, you see a shadow move. It is highly doubtful that you are being haunted, but instead that your guide or guides are watching over you and possibly trying to get your attention. Pay attention to omens, messages, the clouds, feathers, bird song—your fortune is hidden in those subtle messages.

5. **Pay attention to gut feelings and/or intuitive thoughts**. Our guides want so badly for us to learn to trust ourselves. Relying too heavily on others' opinions and ideas, even if it be a professional opinion, can help you lose your own self.

6. **Journal.** Journaling those gut feelings and/or intuitive thoughts can help show you how right on you truly are. Everybody has a psychic ability, and with the help of our guides, the validation of your feelings and thoughts often gives more confidence to trust even more. You can even write down some questions that you'd like to ask your guides. This method is often called automatic writing and your guides can communicate through this means. At first it may seem like you're just typing answers from your imagination, but as you continue to practice this, you will begin to see the difference between your typical communications compared to your automatic writing. Grammar, sentence structure, and dialogue may be slightly different, or it might be completely different.

7. **Meditate.** Turn off the television, your cell phone, and your laptop. Sit somewhere that you won't be disturbed and can shut down for ten minutes. Then imagine yourself walking in a garden. As you get to the middle of the garden, there is a bench. Sit down on the bench and ask your guides to sit with you and have a chat. Ask what their name is. And just as in the automatic writing, don't doubt yourself—just take what you hear. Ask them to show you what sign they give you when they are around. Again, don't doubt. The more you do the meditation, the clearer the connection will become.

8. **Dream.** One of the best ways to meet and connect with your guides is to meet them halfway in a dream state. Before bedtime put the intention out that you want to connect with your guides in your dreams. Do this every single night. It may take a while, but you will eventually see results.

9. **Ask.** When all else fails, see a reputable psychic or medium.

How Do You Know
if You're Just Imagining It All?

Often people will wonder if it is their imagination playing tricks on them just because it can be confusing at first where the information is really coming from, or if it is coming from your subconscious. Some questions to ask are:

1. Does it resonate with you?

2. Is there anything validating that you can go off of?

3. Does the advice make sense to you?

4. Are you receiving results when you listen to what they say?

5. Do your guides stay consistent each time that you connect?

Our guides, angels, and loved ones on the other side try to help us through times that we believe are difficult, but in fact are only lessons to teach us to roll with the punches. The more we paddle our boat opposite the flow, the more exhausted and frustrated we will become. It isn't always comfortable to be put in certain positions and it sometimes takes a lot of strength, but relying on friends, family, and the other side certainly helps release some of the heaviness in the heart.

Remember that sometimes a slide backward means lessons unlearned, but it doesn't mean "game over." And when you are going through something that can't be changed, listen closely, because I am sure your guides and angels are whispering, "Everything is happening just the way it is supposed to."

Meditation

A great meditation to help balance yourself and awaken your senses so that you can connect with your guides is called the Tree Hugging Meditation. And you do just that—hug a tree. You can envision the tree or actually hug the tree, it is up to you! Nature is very healing and grounding.

In your yard, a park, or a forest where you have privacy, choose a tree that attracts you. It might be young or old. Then inwardly ask it for permission to approach it. When you sense the okay, approach it.

Put your hands on the tree trunk. Begin speaking to the tree out loud, if possible, or mentally. Tell it your story. If you feel sad or have some unresolved situation, speak it. Trust yourself to do this. Speak until your story is finished and you have no more to say. At some point or when you reach the end, just rest your forehead against the trunk.

There is no wrong or right with this meditation, or any meditation. Do what feels right for you.

You may feel the tree receive your story and lift your energy upward. Your mind may become still and silent. No thoughts. No sadness. You may enter meditation or deep relaxation standing with the tree. You'll get a sense of the grounding force of nature. It might be the first time or maybe more deeply than other times.

This grounding meditation can show you just how healing nature is and release negative emotions. Nature is a powerful healer.

Be good to yourself. By using a grounding meditation for five minutes a day you will begin to see and feel the results!

If you feel uncomfortable actually hugging the tree, simply close your eyes and in your mind's eye envision a park and a large oak tree and do the exercise accordingly. You may even sense an animal guide standing with you near the tree; the animals, too, have medicinal qualities.

References

Books

Bohner, Charles H. *John Pendleton Kennedy: Gentleman from Baltimore*. Baltimore, MD: Johns Hopkins University Press, 1961.

Boll, Ernest. "The Manuscript of *The Murders in the Rue Morgue,* and Poe's Revisions." *Modern Philology*, vol. 40. Chicago, IL: University of Chicago Press, 1943.

Booker, Christopher. *The Seven Basic Plots*. London: Continuum, 2004.

Broussard, Louis. *The Measure of Poe*. Norman, OK: University of Oklahoma Press, 1969.

Cleman, John. "Irresistible Impulses: Edgar Allan Poe and the Insanity Defense." *American Literature*, vol. 63, no. 4. Durham, NC: Duke University Press, 1991.

Cornelius, Kay. *Biography of Edgar Allan Poe*. Philadelphia, PA: Chelsea House Publishers, 1992.

Cornelius, Kay and Harold Bloom, *Bloom's BioCritiques: Edgar Allan Poe*, Philadelphia, PA: Chelsea House Publishers, 2002.

Dwyer, Jeff. *Ghost Hunter's Guide to New Orleans*. Gretna, LA: Pelican Publishing, 2007.

Hayes, Kevin J. *The Cambridge Companion to Edgar Allan Poe*. Cambridge, UK: Cambridge University Press, 2002.

Hoffman, Daniel. *Poe Poe Poe Poe Poe Poe Poe*. Garden City, New York: Doubleday, 1972.

Jameson, W. C. *Buried Treasures of the South: Legends of Lost, Buried, and Forgotten Treasures—from Tidewater Virginia and Coastal Carolina to Cajun Louisiana*. Little Rock, AR: August House Publishers, 1992.

Kennedy, J. Gerald. *Poe, Death, and the Life of Writing*. New Haven, CT: Yale University Press, 1987.

Merton, Robert K. *The Travels and Adventures of Serendipity: A study in Sociological Semantics and the Sociology of Science* (Paperback ed.). Princeton, NJ: Princeton University Press, 2006.

Meyers, Jeffrey. *Edgar Allan Poe—His Life and Legacy.* New York: Charles Scribner's Sons, 1992.

Miller, John. *Building Poe Biography.* Baton Rouge, LA: Louisiana State University Press, 1977.

Neimeyer, Mark. "Poe and Popular Culture" in *The Cambridge Companion to Edgar Allan Poe,* edited by Kevin J. Hayes. Cambridge, UK: Cambridge University Press, 2002.

Poe, Edgar Allan. *Collected Works of Edgar Allan Poe.* New York: Walter J. Black, 1927.

Poe, Edgar Allan. *Complete Stories and Poems of Edgar Allan Poe.* Garden City, NY: Doubleday, 1966.

Poe, Edgar Allan. *Marginalia.* Charlottesville, VA: University of Virginia Press, 1981.

Quinn, Arthur Hobson. *Edgar Allan Poe: A Critical Biography.* Baltimore, MD: Johns Hopkins University Press, 1998.

Rorabaugh, W. J. *The Alcoholic Republic: An American Tradition.* New York: Oxford University Press, 1979.

Rosenheim, Shawn. *The Cryptographic Imagination: Secret Writing from Edgar Poe to the Internet.* Baltimore, MD: Johns Hopkins University Press, 1997.

Seebold, Herman de Bachellé. *Old Louisiana Plantation Homes and Family Trees*. Gretna, LA: Pelican Publishing, 2004.

Silverman, Kenneth. *Edgar A. Poe: Mournful and Never-ending Remembrance*. New York: HarperCollins, 1991.

Sova, Dawn B. *Edgar Allan Poe, A to Z: The Essential Reference to His Life and Work*. (Paperback ed.). New York: Facts on File, 2001.

Srebnick, Amy Gilman. *The Mysterious Death of Mary Rogers*. New York: Oxford University Press, 1995.

Symons, Julian. *The Tell-Tale Heart—The Life and Work of Edgar Allan Poe*. New York: Penguin Books, 1981.

Thomas, Peter. "Poe's Dupin and the Power of Detection" in *The Cambridge Companion to Edgar Allan Poe*, edited by Kevin J. Hayes. Cambridge, UK: Cambridge University Press, 2002.

Van Leer, David. "Detecting Truth: The World of the Dupin Tales" in *New Essays on Poe's Major Tales*, edited by Kenneth Silverman, 65–92. New York: Cambridge University Press, 1993.

Walsh, John Evangelist. *Midnight Dreary—The Mysterious Death of Edgar Allan Poe*. New Brunswick, NJ: Rutgers University Press, 1998.

Online

www.chretienpoint.com

www.eapoe.org/pstudies/ps1970/p1974204.htm

www.eapoe.org/papers/psbbooks/pb19871.htm

www.eapoe.org/pstudies/ps1970/p1972209.htm

www.eapoe.org/papers/psbbooks/pb19871.htm

www.thefreemasonshall.com/Welcome_To_The_
Freemasons_Hall/History.html

www.gettysburgbattlefieldtours.com/dobbin-house/

www.historichotels.org/hotels-resorts/admiral-fell-
inn/history.php

www.nationalheritagemuseum.typepad.com/library_
and_archives/sons-of-temperance/

www.nps.gov/fosu/planyourvisit/upload/Edgar_Allan_
Poe.pdf

www.plymoutholdvillage.com/old-village-history

www.thereynoldsmansion.com/reynolds-mansion-
history/

www.sonsoftemperance.info/history_us.htm

www.trutv.com/library/crime/notorious_murders/
classics/mary_rogers/8.html

www.trutv.com/library/crime/notorious_murders/
   classics/mary_rogers/8.html

www.visitnc.com/listing/reynolds-mansion-bed-
   breakfast-inn